D0840346

A Two-Hundred Year History of Ornithology, Avian Biology, Bird Watching, and Birding in Kansas (1810–2010)

Thomas G. Shane

To Paul Johnsgard,
Best wishes and
thanks for all the
new horizons since
meeting you!
Tom Shane

P.S. I hope you
approve of the used
of the
your LPCH. He replaced
a Horned Lark.
TS

Abstract

The first two centuries of bird study in Kansas essentially can be split into 50 year intervals since Zebulon Pike's 1810 publication, an account of his explorations. The first 50 years were records of explorers crossing Kansas collecting bird specimens; many were Army doctors. The second half of the 19th Century was a continuation of explorers and those affiliated with museums obtaining bird specimens and the establishment of colleges and universities with faculty members also collecting birds and making observations. The first half of the 20th Century was a period of college faculties primarily composed of vertebrate zoologists who had a few graduate students who studied birds. By 1960, active graduate programs were in place with many professors specializing in taxonomy, physiology, ecology, wildlife biology and behavior which continue to this day. Bird watchers and birders have also played an important role in the study of Kansas birds and continue to do so into the 21st Century.

A Two-Hundred Year History

of

Ornithology, Avian Biology, Bird Watching, and Birding in Kansas

(1810–2010)

Thomas G. Shane

tom.shane@sbcglobal.net
Garden City, Kansas

Zea Books
Lincoln, Nebraska

2012

Dedicated to

Sara, Margaret, Andrea, Christopher, Vivien and Isaac Shane.

ISBN 978-1-60962-024-0 paperback
ISBN 978-1-60962-025-7 e-book

Set in Goudy Old Style types.
Design and composition by Paul Royster.

Zea E-Books are published by the
University of Nebraska–Lincoln Libraries.

Electronic (pdf) edition available online at http://digitalcommons.unl.edu/zeabook/

Print edition can be ordered from http://www.lulu.com/spotlight/unllib

Contents

Introduction

Two hundred years ago a few men exploring Kansas started collecting specimens of the birds they found in the state. These specimens were the beginning of a list of bird species that has grown to be exceptional for a landlocked state. Barrow labeled it "The Culture of Collecting" (1998). That era began to wane when colleges and universities started springing up at the end of the Civil War. However, Sibley still considered the period 1853 through 1903 as a period almost completely devoted to systematics in North America (1955). The Kansas professors at that time worked on continuing additions to the state list, and they also started publishing county lists and notes on life history observations at the end of the 19th Century. Kansas ornithology in the 19th Century and the last half of the 20th Century is moderately well documented in the literature. Our recorded history of the first half of the 20th Century is spotty. I first called it the "dark ages of Kansas ornithology;" however, I then realized that these years were a major transition period that partially slipped into obscurity. Ornithology was not taken seriously by the professional zoologists during that time (Mayr 1975). Colleges had students working with birds, but very few professors were devoted to fulltime bird study. Many of the past professors considered themselves vertebrate or invertebrate zoologists.

It was very common for graduate students under one professor to work with a variety of animal groups. An overlooked case at the University of Kansas (KU) during the first half of the 20th Century involved C. D. Bunker and "Bunk's boys." Historical writings on the period gave most or all credit to the success of graduate students of the 1930s working with birds to Bunker, a KU museum assistant curator (Hall 1951, Johnston 1995). When examining MA theses, it became obvious what was happening through the museum directorship of Henry H. Lane at KU. At least five students graduated with Master of Arts degrees working with birds during that time with Lane as their major professor primarily contributing to the writing phase of their research. Similar events were happening at other colleges and universities in Kansas. This pattern continued until just after World War II when graduate programs started to become a serious component of the academic environment in Kansas. All scientific disciplines underwent a rapid growth in the late fifties, most likely spurred on by "Sputnik," which continues to this day. Large scale research programs, operated by professors and their graduate students, have been the norm for the past 50 years. Kansas faculty members working with birds have come from some extraordinary backgrounds studying under famous ornithologists around the country such as Farner, Grinnell, Kendeigh, Miller, Sutton and Van Tyne.

Ornithology is somewhat unique in that it has a large number of non-academic participants primarily composed of birders and bird watchers. Herschel T. Gier, in his address to the Kansas Ornithological Society convention in 1951, concluded that with the foundation placed by the late 19th Century ornithologists and the publication of field guides such as those by Roger T. Peterson, that some of the amateurs had become some of our best ornithologists (1951). These dedicated people have helped produce and complete some extraordinary bird projects in Kansas such as Audubon Christmas Bird Counts, atlases (neighboring states included), bird feeder counts, the completion of Breeding Bird Survey routes, and the publication of some of their own independent studies. Contributions by this group have been responsible for the majority of the additions to the state bird list in modern times.

Procedures

A cutoff date of 31 December 2010 was used for this historical compilation. The section on the Academic History of the colleges and universities has been placed in order by earliest ornithological activity. An academic institution is usually mentioned in the text by its current name or an abbreviation. This history attempts to include those working with birds except for the fields of paleontology, poultry science and pet birds. The Academic History section includes the professors, instructors, researchers and curators of the Kansas colleges and universities. Their paragraphs include some of their ornithological accomplishments, their research, publications and their students. The various sections have most individuals highlighted in **bold** except for a few long series of participants.

Abbreviations:

AOU	American Ornithologists' Union
CBC	Christmas Bird Count
ESU	Emporia State University
FHSU	Fort Hays State University
IBBA	Inland Bird Banding Association
KOS	Kansas Ornithological Society
KOSB	*Kansas Ornithological Society Bulletin*
KOSN	*Kansas Ornithological Society Newsletter*
KSU	Kansas State University
KU	University of Kansas
MA	Master of Arts
MS	Master of Science
NRCS	Natural Resources Conservation Service
PhD	Doctor of Philosophy
PSU	Pittsburg State University
SC	Southwestern College
TKAS	*Transactions of the Kansas Academy of Science*
WSU	Wichita State University

Early History

The early 19th Century explorers, **Major Zebulon Pike** and the team of **Meriwether Lewis** and **William Clark**, recorded the first two bird species in Kansas: the turkey and the Whip-poor-will (Lantz 1899). The first ornithologist to cross Kansas was **Thomas Say,** who accompanied the **Major Stephen H. Long** expedition and explored the northeastern part of the state in 1819. The following year a detachment with Say descended the Arkansas River valley by horseback. Unfortunately, Say's notes were stolen, but by the compilation of other party members' notes, some approximate locations of bird sightings can be made, especially the Bald Eagle in Barton County (James 1823). Additional explorers during the following decades such as **Maximilian Prince of Wied, Josiah Gregg, Captain John C. Fremont,** and **Lieutenant J. W. Abert** added about 40 new species to the Kansas list of birds (Lantz 1899).

The mastermind of ornithological exploration on the new frontier was indeed **Spencer Fullerton Baird** of the Smithsonian Institution. Prior to the Civil War, he recruited the help of numerous medical doctors of the U.S. Army and associated naturalists to collect birds when the physicians had free time from regular duties. This was also the period when routes for railroads were being studied (Baird et al. 1858). The two prominent names of Baird's recruits who lived in and collected birds in Kansas were **Dr. William A. Hammond** (Hume 1942) and **John Xantus de Vesey** (Harris 1934). Both were stationed at Fort Riley for a considerable time during the early 1850s. Their list of birds included a Carolina Parakeet (Hume 1942). Also working out of Fort Riley in 1856 and 1857 were **Lieutenant F. T. Bryan** and naturalist **W. S. Wood,** who made several large collections of birds. **Lieutenant D. N. Couch** collected birds in the Ft. Leavenworth area from

1854 through 1856. **William M. Magraw** and **Dr. James G. Cooper** collected around Shawnee Mission and Fort Leavenworth in 1857. Several other men were given credit for collecting birds in the KT (Kansas Territory), but some of those men appear to have been outside the present boundaries of Kansas. At that time Kansas extended west to the Continental Divide (Baird et al. 1858).

Many of these Kansas explorers had bird species named in their honor such as: Lewis's Woodpecker, Clark's Nutcracker, Say's Phoebe, Wied's Flycatcher, Abert's Towhee, Baird's Sandpiper, Hammond's Flycatcher, Xantus's Hummingbird, Couch's Kingbird, Cooper's Hawk, and Coues's Flycatcher. The Cooper Ornithological Society was named in honor of J. G. Cooper.

James R. Mead was one of the early naturalists of Kansas. He was a member and president of the Kansas Academy of Science in 1888. He reported on many subjects including birds (Janzen 2007a, Mead 1986) . His paper presented at the Kansas Academy of Science meeting in 1898 on quail being native to Kansas was significant in that he was able to make observations as early as 1859 (1899).

Joel A. Allen, first president of the AOU, made an extremely important expedition to Kansas studying birds and recording populations that are no longer found in Kansas. He also recorded the first bird strike kills of Horned Larks hitting telegraph lines on the Great Plains (Allen 1872). **Elliott Coues** and **P. R. Hoy** also added several species mid-century (Lantz 1899). A compilation of 19th Century newspaper articles on wildlife from around Kansas by Fleharty (1995) gives some excellent examples of the bird populations present during that era. The result of one hunt in 1872 southeast of Fort Dodge, most likely on Bluff Creek, contained one pigeon which may have been a Passenger Pigeon. Over 1,200 birds and mammals were shot for food for the troops stationed at the fort.

The first longtime resident ornithologist of Kansas was **Nathaniel S. Goss**. He, unlike most naturalists of the 19th Century,

was devoted to bird study (Taylor 1932). The first record of Goss'
bird collecting at Neosho Falls was a letter to his sister in January
of 1861 (Janes 1964). He published numerous updates to the Kansas list in *The Bulletin of the Nuttall Ornithological Club*, *The Auk* and
TKAS, as well as publishing some of the first natural history observations on birds in Kansas (1884). He published three editions of
a Kansas bird list (1883, 1886, and 1891); the 1886 edition is the
most usable for Kansas research. Goss' final and largest publication on Kansas birds (1891) appears to contain considerable data
from outside of Kansas. He was a member of the AOU Council
and never missed a meeting, which was admirable in those days
since most were close to 3,000-mile round trips from Kansas.

Academic History

University of Kansas (KU), Lawrence

The early years of ornithology at KU began a few days before the official opening of the university in 1866. **Francis H. Snow** was hired as a professor of natural sciences, where his specialties were in entomology and meteorology. He received his PhD in 1881 from Williams College and was president of The Kansas Academy of Science 1874–1878 and Treasurer from 1869–1873. However, from the first day, he diligently added bird specimens to the museum collection, increasing the Kansas list and continued publishing bird records until near his death in 1908. From those initial bird specimens, the KU museum grew into one of the largest bird collections in the United States. Snow published the first Kansas bird list in 1872 and published his final list in 1903. Joel A. Allen puts in perspective all five of Snow's catalogs in his 1903 review. Snow also became Chancellor of the university and was responsible for the construction of many buildings along with keeping up with his scientific endeavors (Taylor 1932, Hyder 1953). One of Snow's foremost attributes was the inclusion and encouragement of women in science, a policy that was extremely rare until many decades later (Snow 1871). A photo of Snow and his students on a field trip in the Rocky Mountains in 1889 includes four young ladies (Dwigans 1984). **Vernon L. Kellogg** wrote his Master's thesis on Mallophaga (bird lice) under the direction of Snow. He published several notes on Kansas birds including **H. W. Menke's** Finney County bird records (Kellogg 1894). Kellogg ultimately obtained a faculty position at Stanford University.

Lewis L. Dyche was an expeditionary field worker who collected specimens and artifacts in many disciplines. He was appointed professor of anatomy and physiology and curator of mammals, birds and fishes at KU in 1888. His taxidermy work was exceptional, specializing in mammals. His bird papers were part of the beginning of the transition of those who only published papers on additions to the state list to those who also offered notes on natural history. Dyche's papers on Golden Eagle stomach contents (1905) and Blue Jay behavior (1908) were examples published in the *TKAS*. He became the Kansas Fish and Game Warden besides handling his duties at KU (Sharp and Sullivan 1990).

Charles D. Bunker, whose formal education extended no further than grammar school, joined the KU Natural History Museum in 1895 as a taxidermist. He then became assistant curator in 1907 until his retirement in 1942. He published a list of the birds of Kansas (1913). He was responsible for mentoring numerous undergraduates and assisting a number of graduate students who went on to hold notable positions in science (Hall 1951, Dwigans 1984, Johnston 1995).

Bessie Price Douthitt-Reed, was an instructor at KU in zoology by 1918 through at least 1922. By 1922 she had married physiology professor Carlos I. Reed. She published a three part series of bird migration dates in the 1918 and 1919 *Wilson Bulletin*. After reading a newspaper story of an enormous bird kill, she took it upon herself to write the mayor of Gordon, Nebraska to request a specimen; he sent two, and they proved to be Lapland Longspurs (Reed 1922). After moving to Dallas, Texas with her husband she published an excellent note on a Green Heron colony at Lakeview, Douglas County, Kansas (Reed 1927).

Charles E. Johnson received a PhD from the University of Minnesota, and was a member of the KU Zoology Department faculty from 1920 through 1923. He published several notes including one on some Douglas County birds, which also included the first mention of an Ornithology course at KU (1927).

Henry H. Lane was a Latin teacher in Indiana in 1899, took a

Master's degree at Indiana University in 1903, and then accepted a position at the University of Oklahoma as Zoology Department head in 1905. After taking a year off, he finished his doctorate at Princeton in 1915 and transferred to Phillips University at Enid in 1921. He then became Museum Director at KU from 1922 to 1944 (Dwigans 1984). He specialized in embryology and paleontology, with one paper in the *TKAS* on fossil birds (Lane 1947). Although not an ornithologist during the time at KU, he supervised the committees for at least five students working with birds. **Jean M. Linsdale**, a KOS charter member, received an MA in 1925; his thesis was a valuable study of birds in Atchison County (1928). **Eleanor Henderson**, one of the first women graduate students in Kansas studying birds, conducted her MA thesis work in Texas County, Oklahoma. She compared her work with specimens from southwestern KS (1933). **Frederick M. Baumgartner** also received his MA under Lane in 1933, a comparative study of skeletons of juvenile and adult Barn Owls. After he and his wife, A. Marguerite, each received their PhDs from Cornell University, he ultimately became a professor at Oklahoma State University (Carter 1997). **Otto W. Tiemeier**, a KOS charter member, with the help of Bunker and Lane, studied repaired bone injuries in birds for his 1939 MA (Tiemeier 1941). He accepted a faculty position at KSU in 1947. **Malcolm J. Brumwell** made an ecological survey, which included birds of Fort Leavenworth for his MA. Malcolm was killed at Pearl Harbor in 1941, a few months after completing his degree (1951).

A. Byron Leonard received his PhD at KU in 1937 and continued on in the Zoology Department. He was a paleontologist, president of the Kansas Academy of Science in 1951 and had one graduate student working with birds.

E. Raymond Hall returned to KU, where he had received his MA, in 1944 after completing his doctorate under Joseph Grinnell at the University of California at Berkeley (Figure 1), and began the modern era of graduate studies. He was director of the museum and chair of the Zoology Department until his retirement in 1967. Although he primarily worked with mammals, he did supervise four graduate students working with birds during the late 1940s. Hall was a charter member of KOS.

Rollin H. Baker was a KOS charter member and received a PhD in 1948 from KU under E. R. Hall and stayed for a position on the KU faculty (Figure 1). He chaired the committee for **Maurice F. Baker** who went on to become a member of the biology faculty at Southwestern College.

Henry S. Fitch, a KOS charter member, assumed a professorship at KU in 1948 (Pittman and Young 2010). He also received his PhD at U. C. Berkeley in 1937 under Joseph Grinnell (Figure 1). Primarily a herpetologist, he did publish a number of bird papers from his ecological research on the University of Kansas Natural History Reservation (Fitch and von Achen 1973). He directed the graduate studies of two students working with birds, including **Dwight R. Platt** who already held a faculty position at Bethel College.

At mid-century a few gray years ensued. **Charles S. Sibley,** a KOS founder and charter member, and **Donald S. Farner** were both faculty members at KU for about a year each before accepting positions elsewhere. Sibley was the initial proponent of the formation of the Kansas Ornithological Society (M. F. Boyd 1974). **George M. Sutton** was offered a position during the same time period but declined (Jackson 2007).

Harrison B. Tordoff arrived at KU in 1951 and received his doctorate the following year under Josselyn Van Tyne at the University of Michigan (Figure 2). He directed two graduate students and published a *Check-list of the Birds of Kansas* in 1956. He was the editor of *The Wilson Bulletin* from 1952–1954 and then moved to the University of Michigan in 1957 (Gill 2009). He was also a *KOS Bulletin* editor.

Robert M. Mengel took the position of University Research Associate at KU in 1953 (Tordoff 1991). He received his doctorate at the University of Michigan under Josselyn Van Tyne in 1958 (Figure 2). In 1965 he joined the KU Zoology Department. He edited *The Auk* from 1962 to 1967 and the *Ornithological Monographs* in 1972–1973. His paper on the Great Plains as an isolating factor in bird speciation was a unique approach (1970). He was committee chair for four graduate students, including James W. Parker, who returned to Kansas many summers to continue his lifelong study of the Mississippi Kite.

Theodore Eaton was a 1933 doctoral student of Alden H. Miller at the University of California at Berkeley (Figure 1). He was the major professor for the Master's study by Marion A. Jenkinson who stayed at KU working with her husband, Robert Mengel. She was a treasurer for the AOU and an annual award in her name is sponsored by the organization (Johnston 1995).

The arrival of Richard F. Johnston in 1958 marked the real turning point of graduate studies in ornithology at KU. He received his doctorate under Alden H. Miller in 1955 at the University of California at Berkeley (Figure 1), and spent two years at New Mexico State University. He published two lists of Kansas birds (1960b, 1965) and one of breeding birds (1964). In 1975 Richard F. Johnston received the AOU Elliott Coues award with Robert K. Selander which recognizes outstanding and innovative contributions to ornithological research. He became an Honorary Member of the Cooper Ornithological Society in 1995 and was the editor of *Current Ornithology* for the first five volumes. His book, *Feral Pigeons* (1995), with Marián Janiga was a very detailed species account with one unique chapter focused on heavy metals as an environmental concern. He was an editor of the *KOS Bulletin*. Johnston chaired committees of 39 graduate students, including Max C. Thompson who completed his MA and ultimately accepted a position at Southwestern College. Calvin L. Cink took a position on the biology faculty at Baker University. **Galen L. Pittman** received an MA then became the KU Field Station Manager and Biologist for the university, and was a past KOS business manager and Kansas Bird Records Committee secretary. **James D. Rising** received the PhD, and became a faculty member at the University of Toronto. He diligently returned to Kansas to conduct the Baxter Springs CBC for many years and to occasionally make additional studies of orioles in their hybrid zone.

After Hall's retirement, **Philip S. Humphrey** became department chair and museum director in 1967 until he retired in 1995. He received his doctorate at the University of Michigan under Josselyn Van Tyne in 1955 (Figure 2), and then held positions at Yale and at the Smithsonian. His major contribution to ornithology was a widely accepted procedure of classifying molts and plumages (Humphrey and Parkes 1959). He directed five graduate students while at KU, including **David E. Seibel** who accepted a position on the Johnson County Community College faculty (Johnston 1995).

Richard O. Prum arrived at KU in 1991 after receiving his doctorate from the University of Michigan under M. C. McKitrick and R. B. Payne; he filled the position previously held by Mengel. He chaired graduate committees for four students. While at KU he was engaged in one of the liveliest debates on the origin of birds to have occurred in decades which all played out in *The Auk* (Prum 2002). He departed for Yale University in December of 2003.

A. Townsend Peterson arrived at KU in 1993 after receiving his PhD from the University of Chicago under the co-chairs of John W. Fitzpatrick, Scott M. Lanyon and Stuart Altmann. He filled the position previously held by Johnston. His research interests are many with the topic of the geography of biodiversity near the top. Twenty-seven of his graduate students have completed advanced degrees in ornithology and biodiversity.

Mark B. Robbins became a collections manager at the KU Natural History Museum in 1993 after holding a similar position at the Academy of Natural Sciences, Philadelphia. He received his MS at Louisiana State University in 1983 under Van Remsen. He is a member of the AOU South American Check-list Committee and is on the editorial board of the journal *Cotinga*. Mark also served a term on the American Birding Association's records committee.

Robert G. Moyle replaced Prum after receiving his PhD under Frederick Sheldon at Louisiana State University and a Chapman Postdoctoral Fellowship at the American Museum of Natural History, New York.

William H. Busby took a position with the Kansas Biological Survey in 1988, and is also a courtesy faculty member in the KU Department of Ecology and Evolutionary Biology. He received his PhD from the University of Florida under Peter Feinsinger. He is a past secretary of the KOS. He co-authored the *Kansas Breeding Bird Atlas* with John Zimmerman (2001) and is only the second Breeding Bird Survey Coordinator for Kansas since 1967.

Kansas State University (KSU), Manhattan

The earliest faculty member making a contribution to the study of birds was **Edwin A. Popenoe** who helped Dr. C. P. Blachly, MD, with his note on the *Ornithology of Riley County, Kansas* (Blachly 1879–1880). Popenoe received his MA from Washburn University in 1880. Some of his bird specimens are still held at the Division of Biology, however, his specialty was entomology. He was a president of the Kansas Academy of Science in 1892 and secretary from 1878–1889.

David E. Lantz arrived in 1883 and was the most active faculty member in ornithology in the late 19th Century at KSU. He had received his MS from Bloomsburg Normal School in Pennsylvania. Lantz published his bibliography of Kansas birds in 1899. If there was ever a serious gap in the long, prestigious list of ornithological publications in Kansas, it has to be the lack of any additional complete bibliographies over the last 110 years since Lantz's work. He also published papers on the birds of the Manhattan area (1896) and Dickinson County (1901). Lantz was president of the Kansas Academy of Science in 1898 and secretary form 1899–1901. He was the first Kansan to hold a National Audubon office, a member of the Advisory Council, in 1900 (Chapman 1900). Lantz accepted a position with the Bureau of Biological Survey under the U.S. Department of Agriculture in 1904 where he specialized in mammals.

Arthur L. Goodrich joined the KSU faculty in 1927, taught a bird study course for several decades, and published the 1946 edition of *Birds in Kansas*. He also published some of Crevecoeur's notes on birds in Pottawatomie County (1932). He was an invertebrate zoologist who received his PhD at Cornell University in 1938, but his ornithological interests were strongly influenced by Arthur A. Allen while a student there (Shane and Lewis 1998). Goodrich was a founder, charter member, and first editor of the *KOS Bulletin*. He supervised Leon Lungstrom's MS work on the comparative study of the proventriculus and duodenum of three bird species (1946).

M. J. Harbaugh received his PhD in 1942 from the University of Nebraska and was on the KSU zoology faculty from 1929 through at least 1951. He had one student working with Ringnecked Pheasants in Hamilton County, Kansas (Trigg 1951).

A. M. Guhl arrived at the KSU Zoology Department in 1943 after receiving his doctorate at the University of Chicago under W. C. Allee the same year. An avian behaviorist, Guhl spent a good part of his career studying the social behavior of the domestic chicken in small flocks. Edward O. Wilson (1975) stated: "During the past 30 years A. M. Guhl and his associates at Kansas State University have concentrated on nearly every conceivable aspect of the subject of dominance relations." Guhl chaired several graduate committees for students studying avian behavior. He was president of the Kansas Academy of Science in 1962.

Otto W. Tiemeier, a charter member of KOS, obtained his MA at KU under H. H. Lane in 1939 (Tiemeier 1941) and his doctorate at the University of Illinois in 1947 studying the os opticus of birds. He accepted a zoology faculty position at KSU the same year. He had one student working on the ecology of Ring-necked Pheasants in northwest Kansas (Rowe 1959).

Herschel T. Gier, was an embryologist and vertebrate zoologist who started at KSU in 1947 after holding a faculty position at the University of Ohio and receiving his PhD at Indiana University in 1936. A charter member of KOS, he was elected its first vice president and second president (Boyd 1980). He was very supportive of students in the Zoology Department. The coffee pot was always on, and his lab was the common meeting place for grad students of all disciplines. He helped form an active group of birders who started its first CBC in 1949 (Shane 1998). Gier's student John Delphia studied the development of air sacs in ducks (1950).

Robert J. Robel accepted a position with the Zoology Department in 1961 and a new era in avian biology began at Kansas State University. He had recently obtained his doctorate from Utah State University under Jessop B. Low (Figure 3), and started building one of the university's most productive graduate programs. His research primarily included ecological studies of both prairie-chicken species and energetics of the Northern Bobwhite. His most recent research was a decade long study of the ecology of the Lesser Prairie-Chicken (Hagen et al. 2010). Forty-seven students received advanced degrees under his leadership, most working with birds. **Daniel E. Bowen,** faculty member at Benedictine College, Atchison; **Dan Mulhern,** United States Fish and Wildlife Service Biologist, Manhattan (Watkins and Mulhern 1999); **Jeff Keating,** Endangered Species Biologist, Fort Riley; and **Jim Pitman,** Kansas Department of Wildlife and Parks Biologist, Emporia all continue to work with birds in Kansas. His student **Nova J. Silvy** originally from Wathena, Kansas and currently a professor at Texas A & M University, received the highly prestigious Aldo Leopold Award in 2005. Robel started a student chapter of The Wildlife Society, mentoring dozens of undergraduates, and additionally served as a president of the Kansas Academy of Science. He has published more than 250 papers, the vast majority on birds.

John L. Zimmerman arrived at KSU in the fall of 1963 after receiving his PhD from the University of Illinois under S. Charles Kendeigh (Figure 4), began working on Dickcissel ecology, and began a graduate program. He offered the first Ornithology course at KSU beginning in the spring semester of 1964. He published five books: *A Guide to Bird Finding in Kansas and Western Missouri*, with Sebastian Patti (1988), *Cheyenne Bottoms: Wetland in Jeopardy* (1990), *Birds of Konza* (1993), *Migration of Birds*, 3rd edition (1998), and *Breeding Bird Atlas of Kansas* with **William H. Busby** (2001). He was the secretary of the Wilson Ornithological Society 1984–1994 and was the first Breeding Bird Survey Coordinator for Kansas. He is a past KOS president and *Bulletin* editor. Zimmerman was major professor for 15 graduate students, 14 of whom worked with birds. His students included: **John L. Tatschl**, who received his PhD and is now retired from a faculty position at Johnson County Community College. **Elmer J. Finck** and **Greg H. Farley** are both on the FHSU Biology Department faculty, and **Thomas G. Shane**, who completed an MS degree, is currently an ornithology research associate at Garden City Community College.

Fred E. Wilson arrived at KSU in 1965 shortly after he had completed his doctorate at Washington State University, Pullman, under Donald S. Farner. He immediately began his avian physiological studies, eventually publishing 42 papers with his most important paper published in the *Journal of Neuroendocrinology* (Wilson and Reinert 2000). Wilson chaired committees for four graduate students working on the testicular cycles of Harris's and

American Tree sparrows. **Manoj K. Mishra** was a postdoctoral student in his laboratory from 2000 to 2002.

Stephen D. Fretwell received his doctorate under Thomas Quay at North Carolina State University. He arrived at KSU in 1969 from a postdoctoral position with Robert H. MacArthur at Princeton. He completed his monograph *Populations in a Seasonal Environment* (1972) and studied Dickcissel ecology. He is a past KOS president and founded the Bird Populations Institute that was carried on by **Robert S. LaShelle** after Fretwell resigned his faculty position in 1981. Fretwell chaired committees for four graduate students, including **Daniel E. Bowen**, who accepted a position on the faculty at Benedictine College, Atchison. **Sievert A. Rohwer,** after receiving his PhD from KU, accepted a postdoctoral position with Fretwell during which time Rohwer collected much data for his numerous papers on Harris's Sparrow plumages.

Christopher C. Smith accepted a position at KSU in 1970 after obtaining his PhD under Gordon H. Orians at the University of Washington, Seattle. He was committee chair for two students working with birds.

David A. Rintoul received his PhD from Stanford University in cell biology and accepted a position on the biology faculty in 1980. He operated a MAPS bird banding station for a number of years, researched lipid metabolism in migratory birds and also initiated some avian isotope studies. He is a past secretary for the Kansas Bird Records Committee of KOS.

E. Dale Kennedy received her PhD in 1989 from Rutgers University and arrived at KSU in 1990. She and her husband **Douglas W. White** primarily worked on Bewick's Wrens while at KSU (1996). She accepted a position at Albion College, Michigan in 1994.

Jack F. Cully holds a position with the Kansas Cooperative Fish and Wildlife Research Unit. He received his PhD at the University of New Mexico under Jim Findley, who was a student of

E. R. Hall at KU. Cully was strongly influenced in ornithological studies by his MS advisor, J. David Ligon also at UNM. Cully had four students working on birds who complete advanced degrees including **William E. Jensen**, who is now a member of the biology faculty at ESU.

Kimberly A. With arrived at KSU in 2000 after receiving her doctorate from Colorado State University under John A. Wiens and holding positions at Oak Ridge and Bowling Green University. She has chaired committees for three graduate students working with birds.

Brett K. Sandercock arrived in 2001 after Zimmerman's retirement. He had recently completed his doctorate at Simon Fraser University, Canada, under Fred Cooke. He then held a postdoctoral position at the University of California at Berkeley under Steve Beissinger and another at the University of British Columbia under Kathy Martin. Eight advanced degrees in avian ecology have been completed by students under his supervision to date. His major areas of specialization have been on the ecology of shorebirds and grouse (Hagen et al. 2010). He is currently the editor of *Studies in Avian Biology* for the Cooper Ornithological Society.

Outside the Division of Biology, several other KSU professors sponsored graduate bird studies. **Ted T. Cable** of the Department of Horticulture, Forestry, and Recreation Resources received his MS in 1980 and PhD in 1984 at Purdue University. He worked with rails for his Master's research. He has done extensive bird studies on shelterbelts and wetlands while in Kansas, and has now published two editions of *Birds of the Cimarron National Grassland,* which contain very good histories (Cable and Seltman 2010). He has also coauthored and published two bird books; *Birds of the Great Plains* (Jennings et al. 2005) and *Compact Guide to Kansas Birds* (Cable et al. 2007). Cable had one student who worked with birds for his MS degree. **James C. Mitchell,** PhD from The Ohio State University, of the Department of Psychology faculty mentored **Michael Stevenson** who studied the behavior of the Brown-headed Cowbird (1969). **John Harrington, Jr.** received his PhD at Michigan State University, a faculty member of the Department of Geography was major professor for **Judd Patterson's** bird migration study (2008).

Emporia State University (ESU), Emporia

Alonzo Collette graduated from the Kansas State Normal School (now ESU) in 1890 and then stayed on as an instructor from 1891–1893. He was secretary for the Kansas Academy of Science in 1893. He published two papers in *TKAS* on Kansas birds including one on the nesting of the Pied-billed Grebe (1893). Tragically, he died of typhoid a decade later while teaching in Denver.

John W. Breukelman obtained his PhD at the University of Iowa in 1929 and joined the ESU faculty the same year. He joined KOS in 1950, published several papers in the KOS Bulletin and was president of the Kansas Academy of Science in 1945. He was also an editor of the outstanding series of publications, *The Kansas School Naturalist*. He coauthored a paper on the birds of Lyon County, Kansas (Downs and Breukelman 1941).

Ted F. Andrews completed his doctorate at The Ohio State University and arrived at ESU in 1948. He was a charter member, 4th president of KOS, and president of the Kansas Academy of Science in 1958. He, along with H. A. Stephens, did extensive work on Great Blue Herons (Andrews and Stephens 1956). He mentored two students working with birds for their Master's during the middle of the 20th Century, including **Robert B. Wimmer**, who went on to hold a faculty position at Southwestern College.

Richard H. Schmidt, a KOS charter member (Friesen 2000), was employed as a taxidermist at ESU, producing some of the finest quality bird mounts in the state for the university museum which is still open for display. Schmidt retired in 1974, and the ESU Museum of Natural History was renamed the Richard Schmidt Museum of Natural History in recognition of his service to the Biology Division.

David F. Parmelee arrived at ESU in 1958 shortly after receiving his PhD in 1957 (Figure 5) at the University of Oklahoma under George M. Sutton (Winker 1999). During his career Parmelee published a monograph and two books on birds: *The Birds of Southeastern Victoria Island and Adjacent Small Islands* (Parmelee et al. 1967), *Bird Island in the Antarctic Waters* (1980) and *Antarctic Birds: An Ecological and Behavioral Approach* (1992). Before accepting a faculty position at the University of Minnesota in 1970, six of his ornithology students completed MS degrees, including **Myron Schwinn,** who was recognized as an Outstanding Biology Teacher for Kansas, and **Merril G. McHenry**, who ultimately became a professor at Central College of McPherson. **C. W. Comer** completed his MS in 1969 with a study of the Slate-colored Junco on the Ross Natural History Reservation, and then did work for the Kansas Forestry, Fish and Game Commission for two years as the Migratory Bird Biologist. **Eric Prather** received his MS, taught biology at Kansas City Kansas Community College, spent a few years at the University of Wyoming, and then taught at Eastern Wyoming College.

Other ESU professors who sponsored bird research for Master's students include **John W. Parrish,** who received his PhD at Bowling Green State University. He had three MS students including **David K. Saunders** who became an ESU faculty member after obtaining his PhD at KSU, and then became the Biology Department head at University of Northern Iowa. **Dwight L. Spencer,** received his PhD from Oklahoma State University and was major professor for three students working with birds including **Gerald J. Wiens**, a Kansas wildlife photographer. **Robert F. Clarke,** a herpetologist received his PhD at the University of Oklahoma, was major professor for four students studying birds including **Roger L. Boyd** who studied Snowy Plovers at Cheyenne Bottoms for his 1972 MS and ultimately became a faculty member at Baker University.

Elmer J. Finck, a past KOS president and newsletter editor, arrived at ESU in 1989 after receiving his PhD under John L. Zimmerman at KSU, and conducting postdoctoral research on the Konza Prairie (Stapanian, Smith and Finck, 1999). Eight of his students completed their Master's theses on birds. **Dena K. Podrebarac** accepted a position at the KU Natural History Museum, and **Charles D. VanGunday** continued his biology teaching position at Salina South High School, and later became a biology instructor at KSU Salina.

Jean H. Schulenberg along with her husband **Ed Schulenberg,** quickly expanded their interests in birds beyond basic birding after joining KOS when she took up bird banding primarily at their prairie home north of Emporia. There she banded hundreds of American Tree and Harris's sparrows. She held the office of vice president of the Inland Bird Banding Association and also held offices in KOS as director, secretary, vice president, and then became the third woman president for the society from 1976–1978. The Schulenbergs became excellent photographers, Ed with his Hasselblad and Jean with the Nikon. They published a number of bird photos; most noteworthy were those published in Paul Johnsgard's 1979 book, *Breeding Birds of the Great Plains.* When most people were looking ahead a few years to their retirement, Jean returned to college, receiving a Bachelor's and a Master's Degree at ESU in Biology. She then taught Biology Laboratory classes at ESU, was the Biology Laboratory Coordinator for 10 years, and is currently the Curator of the ESU Herbarium. Jean also studied Least Terns (Schulenberg and Ptacek 1984) and Henslow's Sparrows (Schulenberg et al. 1994).

William E. Jensen received his PhD at KSU in 2003 under Jack Cully. He received a postdoctoral position with Kimberly A.

With at KSU and then joined the biological sciences faculty at ESU in 2006 where he immediately started a graduate program with two students completing the MS degree to date.

Fort Hays State University (FHSU), Hays

Lyman D. Wooster arrived at Fort Hays State in 1909 and published a book titled *Nature Studies (Animals)* in 1925 of which almost half was devoted to bird study. He started an Ornithology course for summer sessions in 1924, which became a formal course in 1936. He received his PhD in 1935 from Stanford University under Willis H. Rich. Wooster's student, Olive Falls, was one of the earliest women doing graduate research on birds in Kansas (1933). Wooster was a charter member and became the 5th president of KOS in 1953. He held positions of Dean and President of FHSU (Johnston 1960a).

Charles A. Ely joined the Zoology faculty at FHSU in 1960 after receiving his PhD from the University of Oklahoma under George M. Sutton (Figure 5), and completing a few years of ornithological research on the Pacific Project, a Smithsonian Institution study. He is a past KOS president and *Bulletin* editor. His studies of Ellis County birds led to his definitive modern list of county birds (1971), which contains a detailed history of Ellis county ornithology. He coauthored the two-volume set of *Birds in Kansas* with Max Thompson (1989, 1992). Ely built a large collection of bird specimens for the Sternberg Museum. Upon arrival at FHSU, he began an aggressive graduate program with 23 students receiving Master's degrees on various bird topics. Among his students still active in Kansas ornithology are **Thomas L. Flowers** who completed his MS thesis on birds of riparian areas in different grazing regimens (1979). He is an active western Kansas bird bander who has banded thousands of birds. He not only bands for the scientific purposes, but also uses banding as an educational tool giving hundreds of demonstrations to Cub Scouts, Girl Scouts, church groups and to school children all over southwestern Kansas. He worked for the NRCS where he dealt with many avian conservation issues. He published a list of bird species for Meade County with an excellent ornithological history of the county (1995). **Arthur G. Nonhof** is currently a member of the faculty of Garden City Community College. **John M. Schukman**, a past president of KOS and current chair of the Student Research Fund Committee, continues to work with the two common species of phoebes in Kansas since the completion of his MS (1993), as well as collaborating with other North American ornithologists working on the Cerulean Warbler (1996). He taught a summer Ornithology class at FHSU in 1974, and then taught Biology four years for Leavenworth public schools. **Eugene A. Young**, who is a past president and current editor of the *KOS Bulletin*, is currently a member of the faculty of Northern Oklahoma College in Tonkawa, Oklahoma. His MS thesis was one of the few comprehensive studies of birds at one of the very important Central Kansas marshes (Young 1993).

Four additional FHSU faculty members were major professors for Master's students studying birds at the time C. A. Ely was on the faculty. **Eugene D. Fleharty,** who earned a PhD at the University of New Mexico, mentored two students, and published an excellent book on the wildlife of Kansas in the 19th Century (1995). **Gary K. Hulett** earned a PhD at the University of Saskatchewan in 1962 , and **Thomas L. Wenke** received the PhD at Iowa State University in 1965. Each had one graduate student working with birds. **Gerald W. Tomanek** received his PhD in 1951 at the University of Nebraska and also had one student studying birds.

Greg H. Farley, a past president of KOS, joined the Biology Department in 1995 after receiving his MS degree at KSU under

John L. Zimmerman and obtaining his PhD degree at the University of New Mexico under J. David Ligon. He is currently an associate editor for the *TKAS*, and continues the important graduate program as well as the banding station established by Ely. Twelve of his Master's students have completed their theses on birds to date including work on wrens by **Jamie Timson** (Timson and Farley 2003), now with the NRCS in Pratt, and **Matt Bain** who worked with prairie grouse is now with Kansas Department of Wildlife and Parks (Bain and Farley 2002). **Constance Chen** studied migrant warblers in western Kansas for her MS (2001), and is a coordinator of the bird data bases for National Audubon, including data for Kansas, and **Scott Newland** is the assistant curator for the bird collection at the Sedgwick County Zoo.

Elmer J. Finck left ESU in 2001 to take over as chair of FHSU's Biology Department. He served as editor of *The Prairie Naturalist* from 1995–2009, the journal of the Great Plains Natural Science Society. Three of his ornithology students have completed MS degrees. He is a past president of KOS.

Pittsburg State University (PSU), Pittsburg

Harry H. Hall, who became a member of the PSU biology faculty in 1920, received his Master's in 1929 and PhD in 1932 from the University of Colorado. He was a Kansas Academy of Science president in 1939, and published a paper on southeastern Kansas birds (1935). Hall had one graduate student who worked on an exceptional ecological study of the bird populations of Crawford County, Kansas (Williams 1933).

Theodore M. Sperry arrived at PSU after receiving his doctorate from the University of Illinois in 1933 in plant ecology, worked with Aldo Leopold in Wisconsin (Leopold et al. 1943), and served in the Second World War. He accepted a position at PSU in 1946 where he taught a variety of courses including a bird study class. He was a charter member of KOS, the 7th president, *Bulletin* editor and was president of the Kansas Academy of Science in 1959. He and his wife, Dr. Gladys Galligar, were honored when the Pittsburg, Kansas, Audubon Chapter was named the Sperry-Galligar Audubon Society Chapter (Kreissler 1999).

John C. Johnson arrived at PSU shortly after receiving his doctorate in 1957 under George M. Sutton at the University of Oklahoma (Figure 5). He initiated some studies of Mallophaga (Johnson and Long 1960), was an active KOS member, and its 13th president.

Steven D. Ford received an MA from Indiana State University in 1975 and PhD in 1983 from Purdue University and then became a faculty member at PSU. He has had two students complete Master's degrees working with birds. Ford is also very active with the Sperry-Galligar Audubon Society.

Ottawa University, Ottawa

Howard K. Gloyd, a herpetologist and ornithologist, received his BS from Ottawa University in 1924, taught biology there for several years, moved to KSU to teach Zoology, and obtained an MS in 1929. He then transferred to the University of Michigan. From 1936 to 1958, he served as director of the Chicago Academy of Science. He received a doctorate from Ottawa University in 1942. He published a paper on hawks in Kansas (1925) along with two Kansas bird records in the *Wilson Bulletin*. He was the Secretary of the Wilson Ornithological Society from 1926 to 1929.

McPherson College, McPherson

Harvey H. Nininger, head of the Biology Department from 1920–1930, was one of the nation's leading experts on meteorites. He was also active in Kansas Audubon (Aaron 1925) and published bird papers such as the one helping to conclude the debate about the status of the Bullock's Oriole in western Kansas (1928). He also published a list of the birds of central Kansas (1927).

Baker University, Baldwin City

Raymond F. Miller received his PhD at the University of Iowa in 1923, and was a founder and charter member of KOS. Miller accepted a faculty position at Baker in 1941 as head of the Physics Department. He had spent the preceding 28 years at the College of Emporia where he published some papers on bird photography in the *TKAS*. He was very active in KOS and the local Baldwin Bird Club. In the 1960s (I. L. Boyd 1974), he self-published a set of seven mimeographed volumes of *Biographies of People for Whom Birds Have Been Named*. Miller, along with Ivan Boyd, published a paper on migration records (1947).

Ivan L. Boyd also joined the faculty in 1941, he recieved his doctorate in Botany at Iowa State University in 1944. Ivan was a founder, charter member, the first president of KOS and an editor of its *Bulletin*. He was active with the Baldwin Bird Club and in 1943 established the Baldwin Christmas Bird Count, the longest continually running count in Kansas. He and several other members, including **Amelia Betts**, a KOS charter member and past secretary, and **Katharine Kelley**, also a charter member, were very active bird banders. For many years, he was Director of the Baker University Wetland Research Area, now one of the most popular birding spots and important conservation areas in eastern Kansas.

Roger L. Boyd, son of Ivan, attended Baker as an undergraduate, received his Master's at ESU and his PhD from Colorado State University under Paul H. Baldwin. He became a faculty member at Baker in 1976, and has done extensive research on the Least Tern, Piping Plover and Snowy Plover (Boyd 1981). He continued in his father's footsteps as Director of the Baker Wetlands (Highfill and Boyd 2002). Roger is a past president of KOS and a former vice-president of the Western Bird Banding Association.

Calvin L. Cink also arrived at Baker in 1976 after receiving his doctorate at KU under Richard F. Johnston. As well as continuing the Baldwin Bird Club tradition and operating a bird banding station, he has also conducted research on nightjars, Chimney Swifts and Screech Owls (1975). Calvin is a past president and *Bulletin* editor for KOS.

St. Benedict's / Benedictine College, Atchison

Rev. Eugene W. Dehner was a professor and head of the Biology Department from 1946 to 1983. He received his doctorate from Cornell University in 1946. His dissertation was on respiration in diving ducks and the related anatomy. He was a charter member of KOS, serving as its first secretary from 1949 to 1952 and as its 6th president.

Daniel E. Bowen joined the faculty at Benedictine after earning a doctorate at KSU under Stephen Fretwell in 1976. He served a term as president of the Kansas Academy of Science in 1988. He and his students most recently researched Snow Geese.

Southwestern College (SC), Winfield

Maurice F. Baker was a game bird ecologist. He received his PhD under Rollin Baker at KU in 1952 where he had done extensive work on Greater Prairie-Chickens (1953). He was a member of the SC faculty from 1953–1956, was the 2nd KOS vice president, and an editor of the *Bulletin*. He moved to Alabama where he took a position as leader of the Cooperative Wildlife Research Unit for the Fish and Wildlife Service.

Max C. Thompson completed his MA at KU under Richard F. Johnston, and then accepted a position on the Southwestern College faculty after working on a Smithsonian research project. He coauthored the two-volume set of *Birds in Kansas* with Charles Ely (1989, 1992). He was an Assistant to the Treasurer of the AOU and received the AOU Marion Jenkinson award in 1999. Thompson was the first KOS newsletter editor, a past president (two terms), business manager, and a *Bulletin* editor. He is currently an adjunct curator of birds at the KU Natural History Museum.

Bethel College, North Newton

Dwight R. Platt held a faculty position at Bethel for four decades beginning in the 1950s. He obtained an MA in 1954 and his doctorate under Henry S. Fitch at KU in 1966. Some of his research was on the American Crow while at KU. He is a past KOS president and was the corresponding secretary for 19 years. He published a paper on the breeding birds of Sand Prairie Natural History Reservation (1975). Platt's paper (2002) on the analysis of the Newton-Halstead Christmas Bird Count, was indeed the benchmark for future CBC analyses.

Butler County Community College

William M. Langley, a mammologist and ornithologist, received his doctorate at Arizona State University under Monte Cazier. He accepted a faculty position at WSU. During that time he had one graduate student who worked with Red-tailed Hawks (Cress 1983). He transferred to Butler Community College where he does extensive research on Red-tailed Hawks and American Crows (2000). He involves freshman and sophomore students with his research projects and then gives them the early experience of presenting at meetings.

Robert Broyles received his MS, studying under Karen Brown-Sullivan, from WSU researching the nesting ecology of the Cooper's Hawk (2002), and then joined the Butler faculty as an Instructor.

Wichita State University (WSU), Wichita

Karen Brown-Sullivan, an ecologist, received her PhD at the University of Georgia in 1982. Two of her MS students worked with birds including **Carol A. Fiore**, who studied cat predation on birds (2000) and **Robert Broyles** who studied the nesting ecology of the Cooper's Hawk (2002).

Christopher M. Rogers became a Department of Biological Sciences faculty member in 2000 after receiving his PhD at Indiana University, Bloomington, where he worked under Ellen D. Ketterson and Val Nolan. Previously he held faculty positions at Grinnell College and the University of Iowa. His primary research interest is in the evolutionary ecology of optimal body mass in birds: maximization of nonbreeding fitness. He has had one graduate student complete an advanced degree.

Friends University, Wichita

Alan D. Maccarone became a faculty member of the Biology Department in 1990. He received his PhD at Rutgers in 1985 under Douglass W. Morrison. His ornithological background was most strongly influenced by William A. Montevecchi while working on his MS at the University of Newfoundland, St. John's. He has done extensive work on herons, Canada Geese, owls and shrikes in Kansas. He has primarily published on the egrets of Sedgwick County (Maccarone, Brzorad, and Stone 2008). He has supervised one graduate student working with birds.

Tabor College, Hillsboro

Max R. Terman, an ecologist, received his PhD from Michigan State University and was a biology professor at Tabor. His book, *Messages from an Owl* (1996), chronicles a hand-raised Great Horned Owl that was followed for a half dozen years by radio telemetry.

Garden City Community College

Arthur G. Nonhof completed his MS at FHSU, under Charles A. Ely, studying the Pine Siskin (1980, 1984) and is currently a biology instructor at Garden City Community College. He is one of the few active bird banders in western Kansas.

Thomas G. Shane, who completed an MS degree at KSU under John L. Zimmerman, is a past KOS president, newsletter editor, and Student Research Fund Committee chairman. He was the Cooperative Projects Coordinator for the Bird Populations Insti-

tute, Manhattan; past vice-president of the Colorado Field Ornithologists and Recent Literature Editor for The Colorado Field
Ornithologists Quarterly. His Lark Bunting research for his MS
(1972) culminated in a technical assessment with Sam Houston
State University ornithologists Diane Neudorf and Rebecca Bodily
(2006). He and his wife, **Sara Shane**, were the Northwest Kansas
regional coordinators for the Kansas Breeding Bird Atlas project.
He is currently an ornithology research associate at Garden City
Community College.

Johnson County Community College

David E. Seibel, a past president of KOS, authored a monograph on the birds of Sumner and Cowley counties (1978). He received his PhD under Philip Humphrey at KU in 1988 and took
a position on the faculty of Johnson County Community College
and later became the Biology Department head. He and his fel-
low bird photographers, **Judd Patterson** and **Bob Gress**, have built
one of the largest digital libraries in the state of Kansas, an excellent source of bird photos at (http://www.birdsinfocus.com/).

Academic Trees for a Few Kansas Professors

Kansas has been fortunate to have professors from academic lines originating from some very prominent schools producing avian biologists. They include Cornell University, the University of Chicago, the University of Wisconsin, and the University of California at Berkeley.

Richard F. Johnston, E. Raymond Hall, Henry S. Fitch, and **Theodore Eaton** are all directly linked to the University of California at Berkeley (Figure 1).

Harrison B. Tordoff, Philip S. Humphrey, and **Robert M. Mengel** have origins at the University of Chicago through the University of Michigan. (Figure 2)

Robert J. Robel is linked to the avian wildlife biology lines going back to associations at the University of Wisconsin through Iowa State University (Figure 3).

John L. Zimmerman's lineage goes back to the University of Chicago through the University of Illinois (Figure 4).

Charles A. Ely, David F. Parmelee, and **John C. Johnson** have their origins from Cornell University through the University of Oklahoma (Figure 5).

ACADEMIC TREE FOR JOHNSTON, HALL, BAKER, EATON AND FITCH; UNIVERSITY OF KANSAS

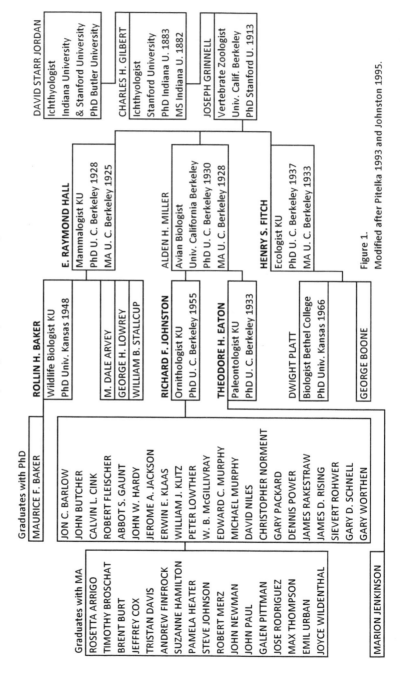

Figure 1.
Modified after Pitelka 1993 and Johnston 1995.

ACADEMIC TREE FOR TORDOFF, HUMPHREY & MENGEL; UNIVERSITY OF KANSAS

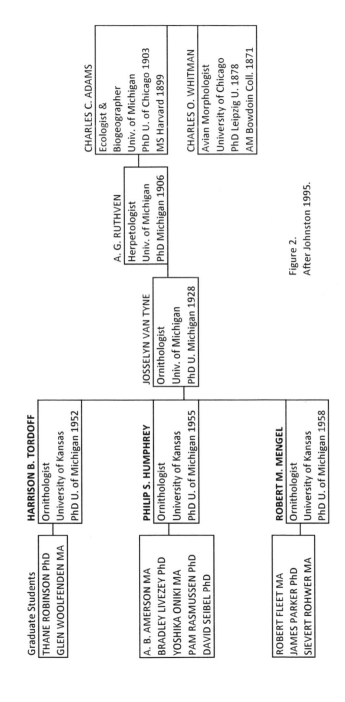

Graduate Students

HARRISON B. TORDOFF
Ornithologist
University of Kansas
PhD U. of Michigan 1952

THANE ROBINSON PhD
GLEN WOOLFENDEN MA

PHILIP S. HUMPHREY
Ornithologist
University of Kansas
PhD U. of Michigan 1955

A. B. AMERSON MA
BRADLEY LIVEZEY PhD
YOSHIKA ONIKI MA
PAM RASMUSSEN PhD
DAVID SEIBEL PhD

ROBERT M. MENGEL
Ornithologist
University of Kansas
PhD U. of Michigan 1958

ROBERT FLEET MA
JAMES PARKER PhD
SIEVERT ROHWER MA

JOSSELYN VAN TYNE
Ornithologist
Univ. of Michigan
PhD U. Michigan 1928

A. G. RUTHVEN
Herpetologist
Univ. of Michigan
PhD Michigan 1906

CHARLES C. ADAMS
Ecologist &
Biogeographer
Univ. of Michigan
PhD U. of Chicago 1903
MS Harvard 1899

CHARLES O. WHITMAN
Avian Morphologist
University of Chicago
PhD Leipzig U. 1878
AM Bowdoin Coll. 1871

Figure 2.
After Johnston 1995.

ACADEMIC TREE FOR ROBERT J. ROBEL; KANSAS STATE UNIVERSITY

ALDO LEOPOLD
Graduate Research Fellowship Representative for the Sporting Arms and Ammunition Manufacturers' Institute 1928 - 1932. Chairman Dept. of Wildlife Management Univ. of Wisconsin 1933 - 1948.

PAUL L. ERRINGTON
Vertebrate Ecologist Iowa State University PhD Univ. Wisconsin 1932 MS Iowa St. Univ. 1926

GEORGE O. HENDRICKSON
Wildlife Ecologist Iowa State University PhD Iowa St. Univ. 1929 MS Iowa St. Univ. 1926

H. M. WIGHT
Wildlife Biologist School of Forestry and Conservation, Univ. of Michigan.

JESSOP B. LOW
Wildlife Biologist Utah State University PhD Iowa St. Univ. 1939 MS Iowa St. Univ. 1937

PAUL D. DALKE
Wildlife Biologist University of Idaho PhD U. Michigan 1934 MSF U. Michigan 1928

ROBERT J. ROBEL
Wildlife Ecologist Kansas State University PhD Utah St. Univ. 1961 MS Univ. of Idaho 1958

Graduate Students

J. J. CEBULA	R. W. FELTHOUSEN
N. J. SILVY	D. H. O'NEILL
G. R. HARPER	D. W. MULHERN
P. G. WATT	J. C. FURNESS
M. P. THOMPSON	S. R. KLINGER
S. R. JOHNSON	T. W. SHUMAN
D. J. DICK	N. A. BARNES
J. M. BRIGGS	J. F. KEATING
C. E. VIERS	M. E. BARNES
C. D. STALLING	D. S. KLUTE
W. B. BALLARD	K. L. POWELL
R. M. CASE	S. D. HULL
R. GARRIGUES	B. L. HENNING
A. R. BISSET	K. W. JOHNSON
T. M. CLEMENT, JR	D. L. OLESKE
D. E. BOWEN	J. P. HUGHES
T. J. BOWMAN	J. J. JOHNSON
K. E. SOLOMON	B. E. JAMISON
G. G. GESELL	L. A. MADISON
D. H. PLETCHER	C. A. HAGEN
D. S. HARAKAL	J. C. PITMAN
S. M. MIDDENDORF	R. T. KAZMAIER
N. E. BROWNING	S. L. BYE
R. L. MEDUNA	

Figure 3.

ACADEMIC TREE FOR JOHN L. ZIMMERMAN; KANSAS STATE UNIVERSITY

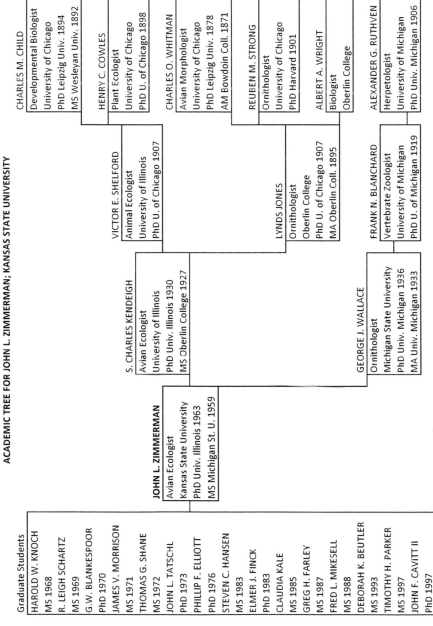

Figure 4.

ACADEMIC TREE FOR ELY, JOHNSON and PARMELEE

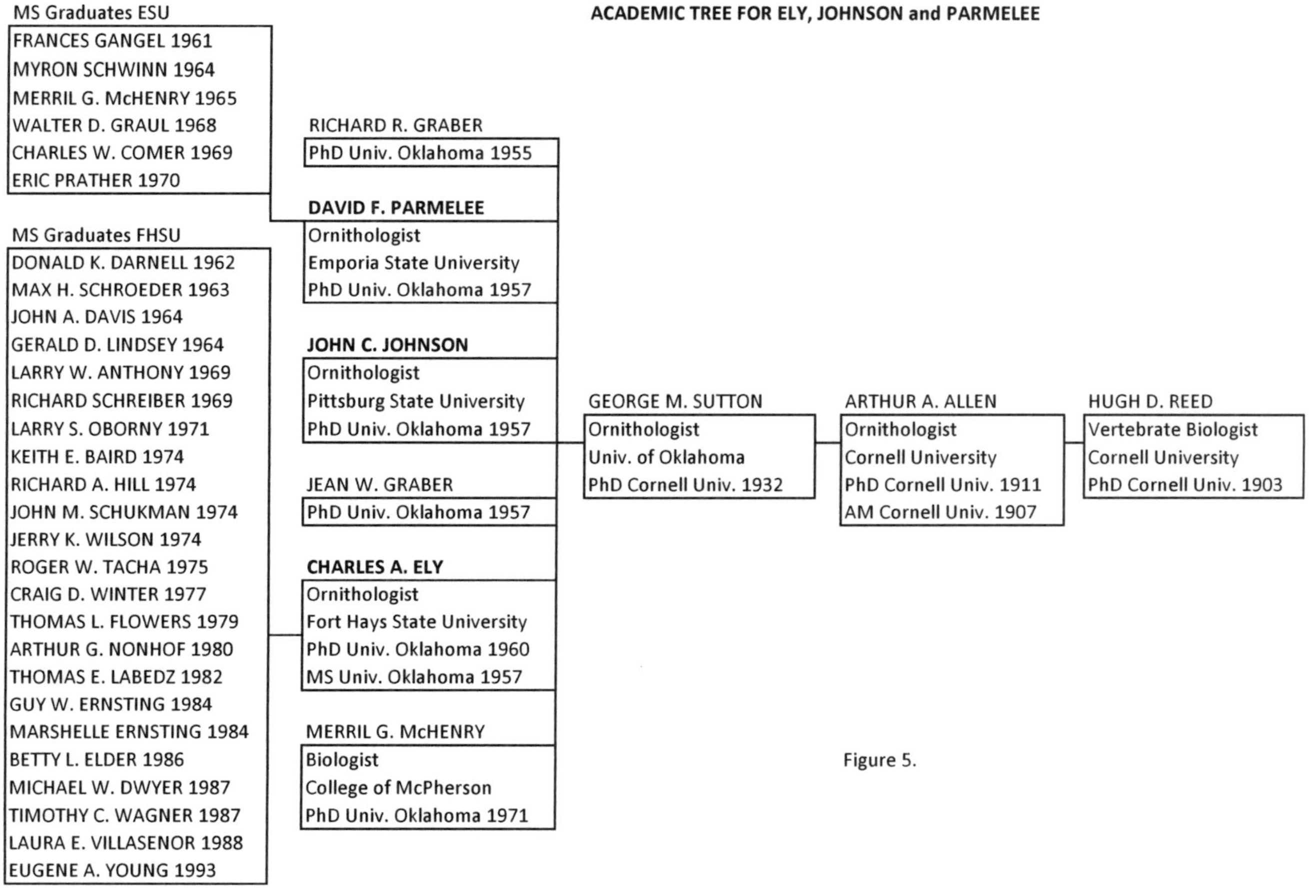

HUGH D. REED
Vertebrate Biologist
Cornell University
PhD Cornell Univ. 1903

ARTHUR A. ALLEN
Ornithologist
Cornell University
PhD Cornell Univ. 1911
AM Cornell Univ. 1907

GEORGE M. SUTTON
Ornithologist
Univ. of Oklahoma
PhD Cornell Univ. 1932

RICHARD R. GRABER
PhD Univ. Oklahoma 1955

DAVID F. PARMELEE
Ornithologist
Emporia State University
PhD Univ. Oklahoma 1957

JOHN C. JOHNSON
Ornithologist
Pittsburg State University
PhD Univ. Oklahoma 1957

JEAN W. GRABER
PhD Univ. Oklahoma 1957

CHARLES A. ELY
Ornithologist
Fort Hays State University
PhD Univ. Oklahoma 1960
MS Univ. Oklahoma 1957

MERRIL G. McHENRY
Biologist
College of McPherson
PhD Univ. Oklahoma 1971

MS Graduates ESU
FRANCES GANGEL 1961
MYRON SCHWINN 1964
MERRIL G. McHENRY 1965
WALTER D. GRAUL 1968
CHARLES W. COMER 1969
ERIC PRATHER 1970

MS Graduates FHSU
DONALD K. DARNELL 1962
MAX H. SCHROEDER 1963
JOHN A. DAVIS 1964
GERALD D. LINDSEY 1964
LARRY W. ANTHONY 1969
RICHARD SCHREIBER 1969
LARRY S. OBORNY 1971
KEITH E. BAIRD 1974
RICHARD A. HILL 1974
JOHN M. SCHUKMAN 1974
JERRY K. WILSON 1974
ROGER W. TACHA 1975
CRAIG D. WINTER 1977
THOMAS L. FLOWERS 1979
ARTHUR G. NONHOF 1980
THOMAS E. LABEDZ 1982
GUY W. ERNSTING 1984
MARSHELLE ERNSTING 1984
BETTY L. ELDER 1986
MICHAEL W. DWYER 1987
TIMOTHY C. WAGNER 1987
LAURA E. VILLASENOR 1988
EUGENE A. YOUNG 1993

Figure 5.

Prominent Avian Biologists with Undergraduate Roots in Kansas

Walter Boles graduated from Emporia State University in 1974 and then joined the Australian Museum in Sydney, Australia, where he is now a Scientific Officer in Ornithology and Collection Manager of Birds. In 2000 he received the PhD from the University of New South Wales for his study on the Tertiary avifauna of Australia. He was a co-describer of a new species, the Eungella Honeyeater, in 1983. Walter is also an Australian representative on the International Ornithological Committee.

Clait E. Braun was an Avian Research Manager for the Colorado Division of Wildlife from 1969 through 1999 working with species such as the Band-tailed Pigeon and the White-tailed Ptarmigan. He received his Bachelor's from Kansas State University, MS from the University of Montana and PhD at Colorado State University. He was part of the team that named the first new species of bird in North America in close to six decades, the Gunnison Sage-Grouse (Young et al., 2000). The species was the first to be split that had not previously been described as a subspecies. He was the president of the Wilson Ornithological Society from 1985–1987 and is its current journal editor.

Ren Lohoefener, a native Kansan, received his Bachelor's and MS degrees from FHSU and his PhD from Mississippi State University. He joined the U. S. Fish and Wildlife Service in 1989 where he later became Regional Director of the Pacific Region based in Portland, Oregon. In 2009 he became the Regional Director of the Pacific Southwest Region, headquartered in Sacramento, California. He administers the Endangered Species Act, the Migratory Bird Treaty Act, and manages 51 national wildlife refuges and three fish hatcheries. He is a past KOS newsletter editor.

Stan E. Senner received his Bachelor's degree from Bethel College in Newton in 1973 and his MS from the University of Alaska, Fairbanks in 1977. Since 2009, he has been the Director of Conservation Science for Ocean Conservancy. Prior to that, he was the Executive Director of the National Audubon Society's Alaska State Office. Earlier he was the Chief Restoration Planner and Science Coordinator for the State of Alaska following the Exxon Valdez oil spill. He was also Executive Director of Hawk Mountain Sanctuary in Pennsylvania and a representative for the Wilderness Society. He was employed by the U. S. House of Representatives Committee on Merchant Marine and Fisheries. Still an avid birder, he has published numerous papers on the ecology and conservation of migratory birds.

Alexander Wetmore, a charter member of KOS, moved from Wisconsin to Independence, Kansas and graduated from high school there. He attended classes at KU where he was influenced by Snow and Bunker, and completed his Bachelor's degree in 1912. He received his MA degree in 1916 and PhD in 1920 at George Washington University. He was the second ornithologist after Spencer F. Baird to hold the position of Secretary of the Smithsonian Institution (Oehser 1980).

Additional Kansas Ornithologists and Birders

Walter S. Colvin graduated from the Osawatomie High School in 1895 and started working for the railroad in 1898. He published a few bird papers in the *Auk, Condor, Osprey* and *Wilson Bulletin*. His best article was on the Lesser Prairie-Chicken in *Outing* (1914).

F. F. Crevecoeur has been referred to as Kansas' greatest naturalist. He made significant contributions in areas such as entomology; however, his contributions to ornithology were fewer in number, but far greater than many professionals of his day (Smith 1931). He published one bird paper (1922) on the Pine Siskin, but his contributions on migration dates for Onaga, Kansas, 1904–1927, were published in numerous articles in early editions of *Bird-Lore* by W. W. Cooke and were the most important for the period. His nesting bird census records for the years 1914–1920 at Onaga were some of the best in the nation (M. T. Cooke 1923). Many additional bird observations by Crevecoeur were published posthumously by Goodrich (1932).

Major Leon L. Gardner was stationed at Fort Riley from about 1926–1927 (Hume 1942). While at the Fort he published several papers in *The Auk*, including one on nesting Great Horned Owls (1929).

Richard R. and Jean W. Graber attended Washburn University when they made their significant contribution to the knowledge of southwestern Kansas birds (1951). Richard was originally from Kingman, Kansas. They both studied under George M. Sutton at the University of Oklahoma where Richard received his doctorate in 1955, and Jean hers in 1957 (Figure 5).

Pete Janzen is one of the most active birders in the state with over 400 species observed and currently has the highest county total for any county in the state with 339 species observed in Sedgwick County. Pete was the second person to have observed 75 species in all Kansas counties by July of 2010. He has been very active in the Wichita Audubon Society as well as KOS where he has held the office of business manager. He was also the south-central Kansas Coordinator for the Breeding Bird Atlas project. His ornithological endevours have included his excellent monograph of *The Birds of Sedgwick County and Cheney Reservoir* (2007a) and he also coauthored *The Guide to Kansas Birds and Birding Hot Spots* (2008) with **Bob Gress**.

Kenn Kaufman was raised in Wichita and became one of the nation's foremost birders (Janzen 2007a).

Albert J. Kirn was most noted for his studies of birds in Texas and Oklahoma. He returned to a family farm periodically in Saline County. He published an excellent list on the density of the breeding birds at the farm (1916), and documented one of the most northwestern breeding locations of the Painted Bunting in Kansas (1919).

Sebastian T. Patti was raised on the border of Missouri and Kansas where he began birding. He leads the state in most species observed with 437, even though he has lived outside Kansas for decades. He has published a number of papers in the *KOSB*, and the *Wilson Bulletin*. He was the coauthor of *A Guide to Bird Finding in Kansas and Western Missouri* (Zimmerman and Patti 1988).

Rev. P. B. Peabody moved many times during his years as a minister reporting on birds from several states including Kansas. He spent a number of years in Topeka and Blue Rapids in the 1920s. His bird observations were primarily published in the *Wilson Bulletin*.

Henry Pelzl was a longtime Kansas ornithologist and oologist. Besides taking a Master's at Washington University, he worked with birds in Belize and at the American Museum of Natural History. He spent his last years in Kansas. He was an intense field man, and when the Kansas Breeding Bird Atlas project came along, he jumped in with both feet spending 250 hours in one block. He donated an excellent bird egg collection to the KU Natural History Museum (Janzen 2007b).

Harry L. Rhodes was a naturalist living in Topeka for 48 years. He was employed as the Deputy Federal Game Warden of Kansas. He wrote a bird book titled *Bird Notes* (1932) which was an accumulation of weekly bird articles published in the Topeka Daily Capital newspaper. He was a charter member of KOS.

Stanley D. Roth earned a Master's degree from ESU and then was a Biology teacher at Lawrence High School for four decades, receiving a State Teacher of the Year award. He was noted for loading one of the school's vehicles with high school students and spending weeks roaming the entire western end of the Smoky Hill River valley studying a variety of animals. His Ferruginous Hawk paper from 30 years of nesting studies is the definitive Kansas paper on the species (Roth and Marzluff 1989). After retirement, he became an adjunct naturalist for the Kansas Biological Survey in Lawrence.

Edna Ruth, Alma Ruth and Ruth Rose were three women who were truly ahead of their time in regard to bird watching and record keeping. Records from their yard and points in Harvey County are extremely valuable for a view of bird life from 1942–1970. All three were KOS members, joining in 1951 (Platt 2007).

Marvin D. Schwilling was the most congenial ornithologist the state has ever known. He not only was very well respected by birders and ornithologists, but was also on equal terms with the hunting and wildlife community. He made a remarkable study of the Lesser Prairie-Chicken when he first went to work for the Kansas Forestry Fish and Game Commission during the early 1950s south of Holcomb, Kansas (1955). In 1962 he became the refuge manager for the Cheyenne Bottoms Wildlife Management Area. He was also the waterfowl project leader through 1976. He then moved to Emporia where he became the non-game biologist for the Kansas Department of Wildlife and Parks. He published 44 papers in the KOS Bulletin (Kuehn 2008). He also published four notes in the *Wilson Bulletin* and the *Condor*, and he was the 9th president of KOS. Other Kansas Department of Wildlife and Parks staff members active in KOS over the years include **Roger Applegate, Ken Brunson, Gerald Horak, Helen Hands, Edwin Miller** a past KOS treasurer, and **Mike Rader** a past KOS president.

Scott Seltman has been a very active birder in the state. He served on the first Kansas Bird Records Committee, served as a KOS director, helped organize the first Kansas rare bird alert system, and was a KOS newsletter editor introducing the very popular "Roundup." He was a Kansas Breeding Bird Atlas Coordinator for southwestern Kansas, and coauthored the excellent *Birds of the Cimarron National Grassland* (Cable and Seltman 2010). Besides birding from a tractor seat on his Central Kansas farms, he has recently undertaken extensive bird surveys for potential wind farms.

H. A. Stephens was primarily a botanist who wrote two excellent books on trees and shrubs for Kansas and the Great Plains. He received a degree in biology and education from ESU and taught school in Atchison for a number of years. During the 1950s he was the educator with the Kansas Forestry, Fish and Game Commission, and toured the state with a large, mobile zoo, housed in a semi-trailer. He worked with ESU biologists who conducted statewide surveys of Great Blue Heron colonies (Andrews and Stephens 1956, Stephens 1980). He was a research assistant for David Parmelee at ESU, working on ravens and shorebirds (Parmelee, Schwilling and Stephens 1969a, 1969b).

Birding and Additional Kansas Ornithological Endeavors

Audubon Society of Kansas, the Kansas State Bird, and the Christmas Bird Count

Kansas was granted a charter in the Audubon Society in October of 1908, the first bird society for the state (Aaron 1925). The first Kansan to hold a national Audubon office was Professor D. E. Lantz of Chapman, in 1900, who served as a member of the Advisory Council (Chapman 1900). A significant part of the Society's mission has been education, and the Audubon Screen Tours (first begun in 1943), have contributed greatly to this endeavor. The 1958-1959 brochure for the Society's Wichita chapter mentions movie presentations by Arthur A. Allen, Roger T. Peterson, and Olin S. Pettingill, who was a charter member of KOS. Currently, there are seven Audubon chapters in Kansas with **Ron Klataske** serving as Executive Director for Audubon of Kansas. With the sponsorship of the Audubon Society of Kansas and the support of the State Superintendent, Jess Milley, 121,191 students across Kansas voted in January of 1925 to name the Western Meadowlark as the state bird of Kansas (Aaron 1925) (Janzen 2007a). The Audubon Christmas Bird Count has been the oldest annual event in Kansas as well as the nation. Alexander Wetmore, a charter member of KOS, initiated the first Kansas CBC in 1904 at Independence (LaShelle and Shane 2000). The oldest, continually running CBC was started in 1943 at Baldwin City sponsored by the Baldwin Bird Club. The Manhattan CBC was started in 1949 (Shane 1998). An analysis of the first 23 years of CBCs published in the *KOSB* was made by Robins and Worthen (1973).

Bird Artists of Kansas

Dan L. Kilby, a longtime resident of Wichita, started his bird painting as a young man at Cornell University in the fifties. While at Cornell he became lifelong friend of Arthur and Elsa Allen. He has published much of his art in American Birding Association publications such as *Birding, Winging It* and the Great Plains Nature Center pocket guide series. Most recently, he published the bulk of the drawings for the *Kansas Breeding Bird Atlas* by Busby and Zimmerman (2001). He has donated much art to KOS for its periodic T-shirt fundraiser and other projects.

Robert M. Mengel was painting and drawing as a young man, and was strongly influenced by George M. Sutton while both were at Cornell (Peck 1991). His art was published in Ralph S. Palmer's five volumes of the *Handbook of North American Birds*, in his own monograph, *Birds of Kentucky* (1965), and more recently, in the *Guide to Bird Finding in Kansas and Western Missouri* by Zimmerman and Patti (1988) and the *Kansas Breeding Bird Atlas* by Busby and Zimmerman (2001).

David F. Parmelee's art was also strongly influenced by George M. Sutton while he was a graduate student at the Universities of Michigan and Oklahoma. He illustrated his own books on Antarctic birds, *Bird Island in the Antarctic Waters* (1980), and *Antarctic Birds: An Ecological and Behavioral Approach* (1992), as well as for several papers on Cheyenne Bottoms birds (Parmelee, Schwilling, and Stephens 1969a, 1969b).

Robert W. Regier is a painter-printmaker who graduated from Bethel College with a BA in 1952, then received his MFA in 1965 from the University of Illinois. He taught art and became professor and chair of the Art Department at Bethel College in 1965. He has made numerous exhibitions of his paintings and prints, usually abstract images derived from nature. His work is represented in the collections of DeCordova Museum of Contemporary Art, Lincoln, Massachusetts; Wichita Art Museum; Fort Hays State University; and Bethel College. After 1984, he became responsible for exhibition design at Kauffman Museum, North Newton, Kansas. Birds are one of his subjects and he plans some art for the KOS T-shirt fundraiser.

Orville O. Rice was a longtime architect in Topeka. He was a past president and treasurer of KOS and was also a president of the Topeka Audubon Society. He illustrated a booklet by L.B. Carson, also of Topeka titled *Introduction to Our Bird Friends* (Carson 1959) with numerous pen and ink drawings along with two excellent paintings. He also painted five plates for *New Mexico Birds and Where to Find Them*, by J. Stokley Ligon (1961). One of Rice's finest paintings is the Bullock's Oriole pair at the nest. His art was also published in the Cornell University journal, *Living Bird*. His pen and ink drawings are still used on the stationery of the Cornell Laboratory of Ornithology.

Margaret Whittemore of Topeka was the daughter of the Director of Art at Washburn University, L.D. Whittemore, and followed in her father's footsteps. She illustrated many publications, including two on birds: *Bird Notes*, by Harry L. Rhodes (1932) and the *Birds in Kansas* edition by Arthur L. Goodrich (1946).

Bird Banding

Frederick C. Lincoln joined the U.S. Biological Survey in 1920 and was placed in charge of organizing the Banding Office. He recruited many banders across the country. Frank Robl, a KOS charter member, of Ellinwood was one of the earliest banders in the state starting in 1923. He primarily banded ducks, which produced a high recovery rate from Alaska to Honduras (1928). The back of his business card read, "Plant a Tree – Grow a Bush – Build a Pond – Kill a Cat – Save a Duck, Frank W. Robl, 'The Duck Man'" (Schwilling 1976). Other early active banding stations include those operated by Ted Sperry of Pittsburg, Edna Stevens of Blue Rapids, W.N. Wilkins, and Mrs. Neil Detrich of Chapman, and William Brecheisen of Welda. Preston F. Osborn of Lakin was listed as banding 1,711 birds in 1941 in a banding report published in the July 1942 issue of *Bird-Banding*. The largest group of banders was at Baldwin City: Amelia Betts, a charter member and secretary of KOS (Kelley 1985), Ivan and Margaret Boyd, Roger Boyd a vice-president of the Western Bird Banding Association, Calvin Cink, and Katharine Kelley (1981), all members of the Baldwin Bird Club.

Additional active banders and IBBA members in recent decades include Wallace Champeny of Oxford; Max Thompson of Winfield; Ed Martinez of Great Bend (1979); Tom Flowers of Meade (1995); Charles Ely (1971), a vice president of the Inland Bird Banding Association, whose banding station was reestablished by Greg Farley in Hays; Mary Louise and Jim Myers of Shawnee; W. P. Conway, Steve Den, Stephen Fretwell, Herschel T. Gier, Dave Rintoul, and John Zimmerman from Manhattan; Jean Schulenberg of Admire, was a vice president of the Inland Bird Banding Association; L. B. Carson of Topeka; Dwight Platt of North Newton; Arthur Nonhof and Thomas Shane of Garden City, C. W. Comer, and David Parmelee at Emporia, and Jerome Jackson, R. F. Johnston and Robert Mengel at Lawrence.

The Birds of North America, Bent's Series, and Palmer's Volumes.

The AOU, Cornell Laboratory of Ornithology and the Academy of Natural Sciences, Philadelphia, initiated a new life history series entitled *The Birds of North America* (BNA) at the end of the 20th Century. The participation by Kansans and former Kansans was exceptional. The majority of the authors completed one or two species accounts. One former KU student, Peter Lowther of the Field Museum in Chicago, authored or coauthored 33 species accounts, an extraordinary accomplishment. No other author in North America came within a third of that number. Current and former Kansas students and professors who authored BNA species accounts include **Alan D. Afton,** #338 Lesser Scaup; **Cynthia A. Annett,** #174 Western Gull; **Jon C. Barlow,** #447 Gray Vireo, and #560 Eurasian Tree Sparrow; **Tim M. Bergin,** #227 Western Kingbird; **Daniel E. Bowen,** #580 Upland Sandpiper; **Clait E. Braun,** #425 Sage Grouse, #530 Band-tailed Pigeon, and #68 White-tailed Ptarmigan; **Douglas Siegel-Causey,** #617 Red-faced Cormorant, and #522 Anhinga; **Calvin L. Cink,** #12 House Sparrow, #646 Chimney Swift, and #620 Whip-poor-will; **John F. Cavitt,** #557 Brown Thrasher; **Scott T. Crocoll,** #107 Red-shouldered Hawk, and #218 Broad-winged Hawk; **Greg H. Farley,** #486 Rock Wren; **Sandra L. L. Gaunt,** #689 Chestnut-backed Chickadee; **Thomas P. Good,** #124 Herring Gull, and #330 Great Black-backed Gull; **Jerome A. Jackson,** #517 Killdeer, #668 Gray Kingbird, #290 Least Tern, #613 Downy Woodpecker, #702 Hairy Woodpecker, #711 Ivory-billed Woodpecker, #148 Pileated Woodpecker, and #85 Red-cockaded Woodpecker; **R. Roy Johnson,** #264 Canyon Towhee, #318 Lucy's Warbler, #357 Elegant Trogan, #474 Strickland's Woodpecker, #529 Zone-tailed Hawk, # 632 California Towhee, and #652 Gray Hawk; **Richard F. Johnston,** #13 Rock Dove; **E. Dale Kennedy** and **Douglas W. White,** #315 Bewick's Wren; **Gerald D. Lindsey,** #360 Amakihi, and #679 Palila; **Peter E. Lowther,** #398 Painted Bunting, #144 Bonzed Cowbird, #47 Brown-headed Cowbird, #399 Shiny Cowbird, #633 Reddish Egret, #466 Alder Flycatcher, #556 Cordilleran Flycatcher and Pacific-slope Flycatcher, #475 Sulphur-bellied Flycatcher, #566 Yellow-bellied Flycatcher, #604 Thick-billed Kingbird, #644 Red-billed Pigeon, #709 Atlantic Puffin, #543 Common Redpoll, #544 Hoary Redpoll, #663 Red-breasted Sapsucker and Yellow-bellied Sapsucker, #638 Baird's Sparrow, #12 House Sparrow, #224 Le Conte's Sparrow, #422 Rufous-winged Sparrow, #676 Black Swift, #595 Forster's Tern, #591 Gray-cheeked Thrush, #590 Arctic Warbler, #319 Black-throated Gray Warbler, #310 Olive Warbler, #454 Yellow Warbler, #579 Willet, #565 Ladder-backed Woodpecker, #555 Nuttall's Woodpecker, and #486 Rock Wren; **Michael T. Murphy,** #253 Eastern Kingbird; **Christopher J. Norment,** #352 Golden-crowned Sparrow, and #64 Harris's Sparrow; **James W. Parker,** #402 Mississippi Kite; **David F. Parmelee,** #10 Snowy Owl, and #329 White-rumped Sandpiper; **A. Townsend Peterson,** #712 Western Scrub-Jay; **Raymond J. Pierotti,** #124 Herring Gull, and #174 Western Gull; **James D. Rising,** #691 Audubon's Oriole, #384 Baltimore Oriole, #416 Bullock's Oriole, #45 Savannah Sparrow, #112 Sharp-tailed Sparrow, and #451 Western Wood-Pewee; **Mark B. Robbins,** #439 Sprague's Pipit; **Christopher M. Rogers,** #716 Dark-eyed Junco; **Frank C. Rohwer,** #625 Blue-winged Teal; **Ronald A. Ryder,** #130 White-faced Ibis; **Gary D. Schnell,** #532 Gila Woodpecker; **Stan E. Senner,** #218 Broad-winged Hawk, and #266 Surfbird; **John M. Schukman,** #374 Say's Phoebe; **Thomas G. Shane,** #542 Lark Bunting; **Thomas C. Tacha,** #31 Sandhill Crane; **Paul A. Vohs,** #31 Sandhill Crane; **Kimberly A. With,** #96 McCown's Longspur; and **Glen E. Woolfenden,** #469 Blue Jay, #228 Florida Scrub-Jay, and #665 Sooty Tern (The Birds of North America 2002).

Five Kansans or former Kansans authored accounts for the Bent's Life History Series completed in 1968. **Jean M. Linsdale** contributed the section on the Green-backed Goldfinch and the Lawrence's Goldfinch and **Jean W. Graber** the Western Henslow's Sparrow. **Richard F. Johnston** authored the accounts on: San Clemente Towhee, Cape Colnett Towhee, Guadalupe Towhee, Large-billed Towhee, Coastal Savannah Sparrow and the San Francisco Bay marsh subspecies for the Song Sparrow; **David F. Parmelee** the Snow Bunting; and **Glen E. Woolfenden** the Northern Seaside Sparrow. The latter three authors not only participated in the Bent series, but also authored various accounts for the recent BNA project.

Ralph S. Palmer initiated an excellent series of species accounts titled *Handbook of North American Birds*, but was only able to complete five volumes. Two former Kansans who contributed to BNA also wrote species accounts for Palmer; **Jerome A. Jackson** authored the section on the Turkey Vulture, and **James W. Parker** the Mississippi Kite.

Kansas Ornithological Society

KOS was founded in 1949 (M. F. Boyd 1974) by a group of professors and businessmen including **C. G. Sibley** (Johnsgard 1998), **Ivan L. Boyd** (Boyd 1986), **L. B. Carson**, past president and treasurer (Rice 1968), **Harold C. Hedges**, past president, (Cooper 2005), **Arthur. L. Goodrich** (Shane and Lewis 1998), **Raymond F. Miller** (I. L. Boyd 1974), and **E. M. Nuss** (Thompson 1998). KOS has become one of the more successful state societies in the central United States. Its energetic and devoted members have played an important part in a steadily growing state bird list, in the completion of hundreds of Christmas Bird Counts, in the completion of the Kansas Breeding Bird Atlas project, and in the continuation of the Breeding Bird Survey in Kansas. The society's newsletter, *The Horned Lark*, with the effort of **Cheryl Miller**, its current editor, in recent times has become an award-winning publication, (http://www.ksbirds.org/kos/HOLA archive.html). The very popular "Roundup" has been published in the newsletter for more than 20 years. It is a report of the noteworthy birds seen in each county for a particular season. It was first initiated by **Scott Seltman** in the September 1987 issue, and has been carried on by 5 other compilers: **Chuck Otte, Chris Hobbs, Pete Janzen, Lloyd Moore** and **Mark Corder**. Many excellent papers and notes have been published by birders, professors and students in the *KOS Bulletin* for sixty years along with the annual "Winter Bird Count," an extension of the Audubon Christmas Bird Count. It also publishes an annual report of the Kansas Bird Records Committee, (http://www.ksbirds.org/kos/bulletin/Bulletin.htm).

Additional KOS officers previously not mentioned in the text of the history include, <u>President</u>: J. Walker Butin, Elizabeth Cole, the first KOS woman president, Celia White Markum, the second woman president, Steve Burr, Jim Mayhew, Roy Beckemeyer who was also an editor for the *TKAS*, and Nancy Leo the fourth woman president; <u>Vice-president</u>: John M. Porter (see Baker 1955), David Bryan, and Marvin Kuehn; <u>all Secretary positions</u>: E. K. Beals, Carl Holmes, Joan Challans, Ruth Fauhl, Charles Franklin, Sondra Williamson, Karen Ganoung, Gregg Friesen, Ruth Broderson, Jane Hershberger, Diane Seltman, Margaret Wedge, Susan Barnes, Mike Stewart, Mark Land, and Patty Marlett; <u>Treasurer</u>: Wilson Dingus, Rose Fritz, Gregg Friesen, Dan Larson, and Terry Mannell; <u>Business Manager</u>: James Barnes, Dave Williams, and Lisa Weeks; and *Bulletin* <u>Editor</u>: John W. Hardy. See M. Boyd (1974) for a complete list of officer and directors for the first 25 years and the KOS website for the recent years, (http://www.ksbirds.org/kos/KOS%20Officers, 1975 to present.htm).

Kansas Breeding Bird Atlas and Breeding Bird Survey

The Breeding Bird Survey in Kansas started on schedule with the other midwestern states in 1967. **John L. Zimmerman** was the first coordinator, who was followed by **William H. Busby** after Zimmerman's retirement from KSU. Kansas has maintained an above average rate of completion for the established routes for this extremely important North American project (Zimmerman 1978).

The Kansas Breeding Bird Atlas project began with suggestions from a few birders around Kansas who were familiar with atlas projects in other states. **John L. Zimmerman** and **William H. Busby** became the project leaders, and a meeting of all regional volunteers and other participants was held at the 1992 annual KOS meeting in Emporia. That summer dozens of birders hit the field surveying 5 km by 5 km blocks looking for evidence of nesting birds. The project was carried out over six years (1992–1997). Results of the atlas were published in 2001 by Busby and Zimmerman.

Regional coordinators for the atlas project included: **Richard Rucker** for the northeast, **Mick McHugh,** KOS past president, in the east-central, **John Zimmerman** for the southeast, **Mike Rader** in the north-central, **Pete Janzen** in the south-central, **Scott Seltman** for the southwest, and **Sara** and **Thomas Shane** for the northwest.

National and Regional Meetings Held in Kansas

The 82nd Stated Meeting of the American Ornithologists' Union was held at KU in 1964 with the Local Committee chaired by **Richard F. Johnston**. The 1972 meeting of the Inland Bird

Banding Association was held at Fort Hays State University and chaired by **Charles A. Ely**. The 102nd Stated Meeting of the AOU was held at KU in 1984 and the Local Committee was chaired by **Marion A. Jenkinson**. The 1997 meeting of the Wilson Ornithological Society was held at Kansas State University with the Local Committee chaired by **John L. Zimmerman**.

County Publications

A few county lists were published as early as the late 19th Century: Riley County (Blachly 1879-80), and Finney County (Menke 1894). County studies published in the early 20th Century include Dickinson County (Lantz 1901), Sedgwick County (Isely 1912), Douglas County (Linsdale and Hall 1927), Rooks County (Imler 1936), and Lyon County (Downs and Breukelman 1941).

Since the publication of Ely's definitive list of Ellis County birds (1971), there have been several additional county publications: Cowley and Sumner counties (Seibel 1978), Meade County (Flowers 1995), Sedgwick County (Janzen 2007a), Cheyenne Bottoms with Barton County (Penner 2009), and Morton County, a 2nd edition (Cable and Seltman 2010). Penner's publication is the only one that conveys the magnitude of the shorebird populations migrating through Kansas, hence the importance of the central Kansas marshes. For an extensive history of the Cheyenne Bottoms area, see Zimmerman (1990) and Harvey (2001, 2005, and 2009). The above publications on Ellis, Meade, Morton and Sedgwick counties contain some excellent ornithological histories.

State and Regional Publications

The major published ornithological works covering Kansas are Snow (1872 through 1903), for a complete list and review of the five Kansas bird lists by Snow, see Allen (1903). Additional publications include those by Goss (1883, 1886, 1891), Lantz (1899), Eyer (1900), Bunker (1913), Long (1940), Goodrich (1946), Tordoff (1956), Johnston (1960b, 1965), and Thompson and Ely (1989, 1992). The publications by Lantz (1899), and Thompson and Ely (1989) contain very useful material on Kansas ornithological history.

Several excellent popular Kansas bird books were recently published including Tekiela (2001), Cable, Seltman, and Kagume (2007), and Gress and Janzen (2008). Several of the many short popular publications on Kansas birds include those by Carson (1959) and Schwilling (1996).

Some additional bird lists and studies from regions in Kansas including reports on migration are: Lantz, Manhattan area (1896); Wetmore, Eastern Kansas (1909); Douthitt, Kansas (1918–1919); Harris, Douglas and Johnson county areas (1919); Hilton, Fort Leavenworth (1920); Nininger, Central Kansas (1927); Linsdale, Southwestern Kansas (1927); Rhodes, Central and Eastern Kansas (1932); Hall, Southeastern Kansas (1935); Long, Western Kansas (1935); Miller and Boyd, East-central Kansas (1947); Brumwell, Fort Leavenworth (1951); Porter, North-central Kansas (1951); Holmes, Cadillac Lake, Sedgwick County (1958); Zimmerman, Cheyenne Bottoms (1990), and Konza Prairie (1993).

Some regional and state works primarily on breeding birds include: Tiemeier, Rawlins County (1938); Wells, Anderson County (1940); Cross, north-central Kansas (1952); Mosby and Lynn, waterbirds for entire state (1956); Wolfe, Decatur County (1961);

Zuvanich and McHenry, waterbirds for entire state (1964); Johnston, entire state (1964), Rising, Cherokee County (1965); Rising, western Kansas (1974); Platt, Sand Prairie Natural History Reservation, Harvey County (1975); and Herbert, sandsage prairie, Finney County (1986). More recently the first state breeding bird atlas was published by Busby and Zimmerman (2001).

Works on the Great Plains covering Kansas include: Johnsgard, breeding birds (1979), and prairie birds (2001); Jennings, Cable and Barrows, which covers all species except rare birds (2005); Fellows and Gress, shorebirds (2006); and Johnsgard and Shane, wintering birds (2009).

The Kansas Bird Listserv

The Kansas Bird Listserv, an online group was co-founded in March 1996 by **Gerry Reeck** and **Chuck Otte**, a past Kansas Bird Records Committee secretary, KOS Newsletter Editor, and KOS President, through the computer facilities at KSU. **Dave Rintoul** came on board a little over a year later. The KSBIRD-L list receives about 3,000 posts per year. The list allows subscribers immediate access to information on rare birds, bird activities and many other events. The arrivals of various species can often be compared over a few days, motivating others to add to the event. This allows for a current picture compared to previous decades when newsletters did not arrive with information until months later. Otte and Rintoul are also co-listowners (along with Laurie Larson of Princeton University) for the global bird list, BirdChat, founded at the University of Arizona by Chuck Williamson in 1991.

State Listing

A small group of birders has reached the milestone of observing 400 species of birds in Kansas. Those to date include **Sebastian Patti** with the lead at 437, **Scott Seltman** at 435, **Mike Rader** and **Mark Corder** with 431 each, **Galen Pittman** 430, **JoAnn Garrett**, and **Ted Cable** each with 425, **Mick McHugh** 424, **Pete Janzen** 420, **Don Vannoy**, a past KOS newsletter editor had 419, **Lloyd Moore** 407, **Chris Hobbs** 404, **Max Thompson** 402, **Matt Gearheart** 401, and **David Seibel** with 400. Most of these dedicated birders invested three to five decades to achieve this accomplishment.

County Listing and the County Checklist Program

The need for county records of all species and the collection of those data were first initiated by **Charles Ely**. The results were often published in the *KOSN*. Well-traveled people like **Marvin Schwilling** kept such records but often for different purposes. **Gene Lewis**, a past KOS treasurer, and **Eulalia Lewis** spent many of their summer vacations looking for evidence of nesting birds in chosen counties; those records were often listed in the *KOSN* such as their summer in Mitchell County (Lewis and Lewis 1976). In the early 1990s, a few Kansas birders such as **Scott Seltman** were some of the first to start keeping checklists for each of the 105 counties. This new method of birding called County Listing has become very popular with many Kansas birders. **Lisa Edwards,** in December of 1999, began making monthly updates of the standings of all the "ticks" made by the County Listers. This report is now carried on by **Mark Land**. The first person to record 75 species in all counties was **Henry Armknecht** on 29 May 2005, and was first again to record 100 species in all 105 counties on 2 May 2009. **Pete Janzen** was the second person to have observed 75 species in all Kansas counties by July of 2010. Birders with more than 10,000 total ticks include **Henry Armknecht, Pete Janzen, Matt Gearheart, Mike Rader, Kevin Groeneweg,** and **Scott Seltman** as of December 2010.

Only a few birders have observed more than 300 species in a given county including **Max Thompson** with 301 for Cowley County, and **Galen Pittman** has 303 in Douglas County. **Scott Seltman** has 308, **Mike Rader** with 308 and **Sebastian Patti** with 331 species in Morton County, and **John Northrup** has observed 304 and **Pete Janzen** 339 species as of January 2010 for Sedgwick County.

Chuck Otte began the County Checklist Program in 1999 by recording new birds for all counties as discovered by the county listers and others. As of December 2009, there were 13 counties with fewer than 200 recorded species and 20 with more than 300 species. Sedgwick County leads with 380 species.

Big Days

In recent decades various birding teams have hit the field in an attempt to identify and record as many species as possible during a 24-hour period (midnight to midnight), with additional rules set by the American Birding Association. Big Days are run in all months, and teams most often consist of two to four observers. May is the golden month when the greatest efforts are made. The first official attempt in Kansas was made on 11 May 1984 by **Chris Hobbs** and **Mick McHugh** with an exceptional list of 172 species. On 12 May 1991 a team composed of **Chris Hobbs, Mick McHugh, Sebastian Patti,** and **Galen Pittman** was able to reach the 200 species mark for the first time. The premier Big Day occurred on 13 May 2002 when **Mark Robbins, Roger McNeill,** and **Mike Rader** located 225 species in 24 hours of nonstop birding. This was an amazing feat in that it tied New Jersey for an all time 3rd place, topped by Texas and California with the advantage of oceans (Rader 2002).

Big Years

National Big Years have been attempted by numerous North American birders including Wichita's **Kenn Kaufman** who recorded 671 species in 1973. Big Years involve a yearlong attempt to find as many birds in North America as they can from January through December. Several Kansas birders have attempted some very successful Big Years within the borders of Kansas. **Scott Seltman** was the first person to break 300 species in a Kansas Big Year with a total of 301 in 1985. In 1990, **Galen L. Pittman** (1991) completed a Kansas Big year with 327 species. **Mike Rader** (1999) recorded 339 species in 1998 and **Chet Gresham** (2001a, 2001b) reached a total of 358 species in 2000. The totals are not comparable due to the splitting done by the AOU Checklist Committee.

Conclusions

I am certain no one outside the field of history ever plans to do historical research. However, it is one of those topics that reaches out and grabs a person. After seeing the academic tree prepared for Grinnell and Miller (Pitelka 1993), I became slightly interested and decided to prepare an academic tree for John L. Zimmerman, his students and academic ancestors. This was done for Zimmerman's retirement luncheon with current and former graduate students held at the 1997 Wilson Ornithological Society meeting at KSU. After Richard F. Johnston published an extensive amount of history on KU ornithology in 1995, I thought a project of this size would be feasible. With Johnston's excellent foundation on KU, my exposure to KSU while working on two degrees, my access to faculty and students from FHSU and ESU at KOS annual meetings, I had enough facts to get started. Dr. Johnston laid one side of this historical foundation, and I hope I have now completed the other sides. The Kansas ornithological community will be able to publish or report additional historical details that will be discovered and compiled for future histories.

If a suggestion for future historical research on the study of birds in Kansas is needed, the first should be the ornithologists and bird studies of the first half of the 20th Century. This topic would be great for an undergraduate project. It was my intent to primarily compile the published literature. Hence, the history of the first half of the 20th Century is not complete, nor has it been in other histories. The electronic library cataloging systems of each university provided a giant step forward. Hopefully, the electronic indexing will improve over the next few decades. I would appreciate any additional information on overlooked people or topics omitted in case I, or someone else, might write a future supplement on this amazing state, so lightly populated yet one that has accomplished so much in the study of birds during its first 200 years.

Acknowledgments

I thank Debra Bolton, Roger Boyd, Barbara Campbell, Dan LaShelle, Eugenia Eberhart, Thomas Flowers, Sebastian Patti, David Rintoul, Jean Schulenberg, Janice Urie, and Eugene Young for reading all or sections and providing suggestions on the manuscript. A special thanks is due the Saffell Library staff at the Garden City Community College; Trent Smith, Carol Heinemann, Lisa Gleason, and Kathy Winter, for their help in ordering dozens of interlibrary loans for this study; and to my wife, Sara, for her patience and love in tolerating stacks, piles and avalanches of books, journals, reprints, interlibrary loans and file folders from one end of the house to the other.

For helpful input I thank: (KU) William H. Busby, Galen Pittman, Richard O. Prum, and A. Townsend Peterson; (KSU) Jack F. Cully, David A. Rintoul, Robert J. Robel, Brett K. Sandercock, Christopher C. Smith, Fred E. Wilson, and John L. Zimmerman; (FHSU) Charles A. Ely, Elmer J. Finck, and Greg H. Farley; (ESU) C. W. Comer, William E. Jensen, Joy Keown, and Dan Larson; (Baker U) Roger L. Boyd, and Calvin L. Cink; (Butler CCC) William M. Langley; (Friends U) Alan D Maccarone; (other ornithologists) Chet Gresham, Pete Janzen, Barry Jones, Dan Kilby, Chuck Otte, Mike Rader, Stan Roth, and Scott Seltman.

For considerable help with research I thank, Thuy Cao, Delia Hernandez, and Dan LaShelle, and to Jim Mayhew for the much used copy of Baird, Cassin and Lawrence. A special thanks to Janet Hinshaw of the Wilson Ornithological Society Library at the University of Michigan for assistance.

Literature Cited

Aaron, M. 1925. The Audubon Society of Kansas, and the election of the state bird. Collections of the Kansas Historical Society. 16: 597–606.

Allen, J.A. 1872. Notes of an ornithological reconnaissance in portions of Kansas, Colorado, Wyoming, and Utah. Pt. 2. Bull. Mus. Comp. Zool. 3(6): 113–183.

Allen, J. A. 1903. Snow's catalog of Kansas birds. Auk 20(3): 317.

Andrews, T. F., and H. A. Stephens. 1956. Notes on colonies of Great Blue Heron in Kansas. Kansas Ornithol. Soc. Bull. 7(4): 17–18.

Baird, S. F., J. Cassin, and G. N. Lawrence. 1858. Reports of explorations and surveys to ascertain the most practicable and economic route for a railroad from the Mississippi river to the Pacific ocean, made under the direction of the secretary of war in 1853-6, according to acts of congress of March 3, 1853, May 31, 1854, and August 5, 1854. Vol. IX. A. O. P. Nicholson, Washington, D.C. 1005 pp.

Bain, M. R., and G. H. Farley. 2002. Display by apparent hybrid prairie-chickens in a zone of geographic overlap. Condor 104(3): 683–687.

Baker, M. F. 1953. Prairie Chickens of Kansas. Univ. Kansas Mus. Nat. Hist. and State Biological Survey of Kansas, Misc. Publ. No. 5, pp 1–68.

Baker, M. 1955. In Memoriam: John M. Porter, M. D. Kansas Ornithol. Soc. Bull. 6(3): 11–12.

Barrow, M. V., Jr. 1998. A Passion for Birds: American Ornithology after Audubon. Princeton University Press. 326 pp.

Blachly, C. P. 1879-1880. Ornithology of Riley County, Kansas. Trans. Kansas Acad. Sci. 7:102–110

Boyd, I. L. 1974. In Memoriam: Dr. Raymond F. Miller. Kans. Ornithol. Soc. Bull. 25(4): 25–26.

Boyd, I. L. 1980. In Memoriam: Herschel T. Gier. Kansas Ornithol. Soc. Bull. 31(1): 16.

Boyd, M. F. 1974. History of the Kansas Ornithological Society. Kansas Ornithol. Soc. Bull. 25:9–16.

Boyd, R. L. 1972. Breeding biology of the Snowy Plover at Cheyenne Bottoms Waterfowl Management Area, Barton County, Kansas. M.S. thesis, Kansas State Teachers College, Emporia, Kansas. 86 pp.

Boyd, R. L. 1981. Distribution and abundance of Snowy Plovers in Kansas and northern Oklahoma. Kansas Ornithol. Soc. Bull. 32(2): 25–28.

Boyd, R. L. 1986. In Memoriam: Ivan L. Boyd. Kansas Ornithol. Soc. Bull. 37(2): 30–31.

Broyles, R. B. 2002. The nesting ecology of the Cooper's Hawk, *Accipiter cooperii*, in south-central Kansas. M. S. thesis, Wichita State University. 80 pp.

Brumwell, M. J. 1951. An ecological survey of the Fort Leavenworth Military Reservation. American Mid. Nat. 45(1): 187–231.

Bunker, C. 1913. The birds of Kansas. Kansas Univ. Sci. Bull. 7(5): 137–158.

Busby, W. H., and J. L. Zimmerman. 2001. Kansas Breeding Bird Atlas. University Press of Kansas, Lawrence. 466 pp.

Cable, T. T., and S. Seltman. 2010. Birds of the Cimarron National Grassland, 2nd edition, 1st printing. Kansas Agricultural Experiment Station publication number 10-390-B. 152 pp.

Cable, T. T., S. Seltman, and K. Kagume. 2007. Compact Guide to Kansas Birds. Lone Pine Publishing, Auburn, Washington. 240 pp.

Carson, L. B. 1959. Introduction to Our Bird Friends. Stauffer Publications, Topeka. 54 pp.

Carter, W. A. 1997. In Memoriam: Frederick M. Baumgartner, 1910–1996. Auk 114(3): 500.

Chapman, F. M. 1900. For Students and teachers. Bird Lore. 2: 12–13.

Chen, C. Y. 2001. Devising a catchability index incorporating weather to re-evaluate population trends of migratory warblers in western Kansas. M. S. thesis, Fort Hays State University, Hays, Kansas. 47 pp. Online: http://contentcat.fhsu.edu/cdm/singleitem/collection/thesis/id/656/rec/8

Cink, C. L. 1975. Population densities of Screech Owls in northeastern Kansas. Kansas Ornithol. Soc. Bull. 26(3): 13–16.

Collette, A. M. 1893. Nesting of the Pied-billed Grebe. Trans. Kansas Acad. Sci. 13: 49–50.

Colvin, W. S. 1914. The Lesser Prairie Hen. Outing 63(5): 608–614.

Comer, C. W. 1969. Winter Activities of the Slate-colored Junco on the Ross Natural History Reservation. M. S. thesis, Kansas State Teachers College, Emporia, Kansas. 45 pp.

Cooke, M. T. 1923. Report on Bird Censuses in the United States 1916 to 1920. U. S. Dept. Agric. Bulletin 1165. Washington D. C. 36 pp.

Cooper, M. 2005. In Memoriam: Harold Hedges. Kansas Ornithol. Soc. Bull. 56(2): 24.

Cress, G. A. 1983. Growth and productivity of Red-tailed Hawks (*Buteo jamaicensis*) in south-central, Kansas. M. S. thesis, Wichita State University. 124 pp.

Crevecoeur, F. F. 1922. A new nesting record for the Pine Siskin. Trans. Kansas Acad. Sci. 30: 376.

Cross, F. C. 1952. Nesting birds of North-central Kansas. Trans. Kansas Acad. Sci. 55(1): 120–125.

Delphia, J. M. 1950. The development of airsacs in ducks. M.S. Thesis, Kansas St. College, Manhattan. 44 pp.

Douthitt, B. P. 1918–1919. Migration records for Kansas Birds. Wilson Bull. 30(1):100–111, 31(2):6–20, and 31(2): 45–52.

Downs, T., and J. Breukelman. 1941. Birds of Lyon County and vicinity. Trans. Kansas Acad. Sci. 44: 389–399.

Dwigans, C. M. 1984. A guide to the Museum of Natural History:

The University of Kansas. University of Kansas printing service, Lawrence. 64 pp.

Dyche, L. L. 1905. The Golden Eagle. Trans. Kansas Acad. Sci. 19: 179–181.

Dyche, L. L. 1908. Some observations on the food habits of the blue jay. Trans. Kansas Acad. Sci. 21: 130–137.

Ely, C. 1971. A history and distributional list of Ellis County, Kansas, birds. Fort Hays Studies, New Series, Science Series no. 9. 115 pp.

Eyer, B. F. 1900. Birds of Kansas. Crane and Company, Publishers, Topeka. 150 pp.

Falls, O. 1933. An analysis of the habitat distribution of the vertebrate fauna of a stream-bank association in western Kansas. M. S. Thesis, Fort Hays State College. 150 pp. Online: http://cdm15732.contentdm.oclc.org/cdm/singleitem/collection/thesis/id/929/rec/5

Fellows, S., and B. Gress. 2006. A pocket guide to Great Plains shorebirds. Great Plains Nature Center, Wichita, Kansas.

Fiore, C. A., and K. Brown-Sullivan. 2000. Domestic cat (*Felis catus*) predation of birds in an urban environment. Online: http://www.carolfiore.com/Article.html

Fitch, H. S., and P. von Achen. 1973. Yellow-billed Cuckoo nesting at University of Kansas Natural History Reservation. Kansas Ornithol. Soc. Bull. 24(2): 12–15.

Fleharty, E. D. 1995. Wild animals and settlers on the Great Plains. Univ. Oklahoma Press. 316 pp.

Flowers, T. L. 1979. Avian communities of some grazed and ungrazed riparian habitats in Ellis County, Kansas. M.S. Thesis, Fort Hays State University. 30 pp. Online: http://contentcat.fhsu.edu/cdm/singleitem/collection/thesis/id/1001/rec/1

Flowers, T. L. 1995. A history and distributional list of Meade County, Kansas birds. Flowers Enterprises, Meade, Kansas. 148 pp.

Fretwell, S. D. 1972. Populations in a seasonal environment. Monographs in Population Biology No. 5. Princeton. 217 pp.

Friesen, G. 2000. In Memoriam: Richard H. Schmidt (1909–2000). Kansas Ornithol, Soc. Bull. 51(4): 35–37.

Gardner, L. L. 1929. The nesting of the Great Horned Owl. Auk 46: 58–69.

Gier, H. T. 1951. Ornithology – Popular and Scientific. Kansas Ornithol. Bull. 2(2): 13.

Gill, F. B. 2009. In Memoriam: Harrison Bruce Tordoff, 1923–2008. Auk 126(2): 463–465.

Gloyd, H. K. 1925. Field studies of the diurnal raptores of eastern and central Kansas. Wilson Bull. 37(3): 133–149.

Goodrich, A. L. 1932. Crevecoeur's notes on birds in Pottawatomie County, Kansas. Trans. Kansas Acad. Sci. 35: 85–92.

Goodrich, A. L. 1946. Birds in Kansas. Report of the Kansas State Board of Agric., June 1945. 340 pp.

Goss, N. S. 1883. A catalogue of the birds of Kansas. Kansas Publication House, Topeka, Kansas. 37 pp.

Goss, N. S. 1884. Notes on the nesting habits of the Yellow-throated Vireo (*Lanivireo flavifrons*). Auk 1(2): 124–126.

Goss, N. S. 1886. A Revised Catalogue of the Birds of Kansas. Kansas Publication House, Topeka, Kansas. 76 pp.

Goss, N. S. 1891. History of the Birds of Kansas. Geo. W. Crane and Co., Topeka, Kansas. 692 pp.

Graber, R., and J. Graber. 1951. Notes on the birds of southwestern Kansas. Trans. Kansas Acad. Sci. 54(2): 145–174.

Gresham, C. 2001a. 13 Ways of Looking at a blackbird: Reflections of a Big Year, I. The Horned Lark 28(1): 21–22.

Gresham, C. 2001b. 13 Ways of Looking at a blackbird: Reflections of a Big Year, II. The Horned Lark 28(2): 15–16.

Gress, B., and P. Janzen. 2008. The Guide to Kansas Birds and Birding Hot Spots. University Press of Kansas, Lawrence. 354 pp.

Hagen, C. A., J. C. Pitman, B. K. Sandercock, D. H. Wolfe, R. J. Robel, R. D. Applegate, and S. J. Oyler-McCance. 2010. Regional variation in mtDNA of the Lesser Prairie-Chicken. Condor 112(1): 29–37.

Hall, E. R. 1951. Charles Dean Bunker: 1870–1948. Univ. Kansas Mus. Nat. Hist., Misc. Publ. No. 3: 1–11.

Hall, H. H. 1935. The birds of southeastern Kansas, with migration dates. Trans. Kansas Acad. Sci. 38: 311–315.

Harris, H. 1919. Birds of the Kansas City region. Trans. Acad. Sci. St. Louis 23(8): 213–371.

Harris, H. 1934. Notes on the Xantus tradition. Condor 36: 191–201.

Harvey, D. S. 2001. Creating a "Sea of Galilee": The rescue of Cheyenne Bottoms Wildlife Area, 1927–1930. Kansas History 24(1): 2–17.

Harvey, D. 2005. Developing a "Grand Lake" in central Kansas: The Lake Koen Navigation, Reservoir, and Irrigation Company. J. of the West 44(2): 81–89.

Harvey, D. S. 2009. Learning the hard way: Early water control projects at Cheyenne Bottoms Wildlife Area. Kansas History 32(3): 186–203.

Henderson, E. 1933. Birds and mammals of Texas County, Oklahoma. M. A. thesis, University of Kansas. 329 pp.

Herbert, L. 1986. The breeding birds of a sandsage prairie. Kansas Ornithol. Soc. Bull. 37(4): 41–42.

Highfill, K. M., and R. L. Boyd. 2002. Successful nesting by Barn Owls in a nesting box in the Baker Wetlands, Lawrence, Kansas. Kansas Ornithol. Soc. Bull. 53(3): 33–36.

Hilton, D. C. 1920. Notes on the Birds of the Fort Leavenworth Reservation, Kansas. Wilson Bull. 32(3): 80–86.

Holmes, C. S. 1958. Check-list of Summer Birds of Cadillac Lake, Wichita, Sedgwick County, Kansas. Kansas Ornithol. Soc. Bull. 9(2): 12–13.

Hume, E. E. 1942. Ornithologists of the United States Army Medical Corps. Johns Hopkins Press, Baltimore. 583 pp.

Humphrey, P. S., and K. C. Parkes. 1959. An approach to the study of molts and plumages. Auk 76(1): 1-31.

Hyder, C. K. 1953. Snow of Kansas: The life of Francis Huntington Snow with extracts from his journals and letters. Univ. Kansas Press, Lawrence. 296 pp.

Imler, R. H. 1936. An annotated list of the birds of Rooks County, Kansas and vicinity. Trans. Kansas Acad. Sci. 39: 295-312.

Isely, D. 1912. A list of the birds of Sedgwick County, Kansas. Auk 29(1): 25-44.

Jackson, J. A. 2007. George Miksch Sutton: Artist, Scientist, and Teacher. Univ. Oklahoma Press. 238 pp.

James, E. 1823. Account of an expedition from Pittsburgh to the Rocky Mountains, performed in the years 1819 and 1820; by order of the Hon. J. C. Calhoun, Secretary of War: under the command of Major Stephen H. Long, Mr. T. Say, other gentlemen of the exploring party. 2 vols. 622 pp. Philadelphia: H. C. Carey and J. Lea.

Janes, W. J. 1964. The Goss Ornithological Collection - A centennial. Kansas Ornithol. Soc. Bull. 15: 9-12.

Janzen, P. 2007a. The birds of Sedgwick County and Cheney Reservoir. Kansas Ornithol. Soc. Monograph 1. 118 pp.

Janzen, P. 2007b. Remembering and honoring Henry Pelzl. The Horned Lark 34(1): 3-4.

Jennings, B., T. T. Cable, and R. Burrows. 2005. Birds of the Great Plains. Lone Pine Publishing. 384 pp.

Johnsgard, P. A. 1979. Birds of the Great Plains. Univ. of Nebraska Press, Lincoln. 539 pp.

Johnsgard, P. A. 1998. In Memoriam: Charles G. Sibley. Nebraska Bird Rev. 66(2): 68-69.

Johnsgard, P. A. 2001. Prairie Birds: Fragile Splendor in the Great Plains. University Press of Kansas. 331 pp.

Johnsgard, P. A., and T. G. Shane. 2009. Four decades of Christmas Bird Counts in the Great Plains: Ornithological evidence of a changing climate. UNL DigitalCommons, Papers in Ornithology, University of Nebraska–Lincoln Libraries. Online: http://digitalcommons.unl.edu/biosciornithology/46

Johnson, C. E. 1927. Notes on some less common birds of Douglas County, Kansas. Wilson Bull. 39(3): 156–158.

Johnson, J. C., and C. A. Long. 1960. Common Grackle heavily infested with Mallophaga. Wilson Bull. 72(1): 107.

Johnston, R. F. 1960a. Obituary. Kansas Ornithol. Soc. Bull. 11(1): 8.

Johnston, R. F. 1960b. Directory to the bird-life of Kansas. Univ. Kansas Mus. Nat. Hist. Misc. Publ. No. 23, pp. 1–69.

Johnston, R. F. 1964. The breeding birds of Kansas. Univ. Kansas publ. Mus. Nat Hist. 12(14): 575–655.

Johnston, R. F. 1965. A directory to the birds of Kansas. Univ. Kansas Mus. Nat. Hist. Misc. Publ. No. 41, pp. 1–67.

Johnston, R. F. 1995. Ornithology at the University of Kansas. 95–112. In W. E. Davis Jr. and J. A. Jackson (eds.). Contributions to the History of North American Ornithology. Memoirs of the Nuttall Ornithological Club, No. 12 Cambridge, Massachusetts. Online: http://ornithology.biodiversity.ku.edu/sites/default/files/ku-ornithology-history.pdf

Johnston, R. F., and M. Janiga. 1995. Feral Pigeons. Oxford University Press. 320 pp.

Kelley, K. B. 1985. In Memoriam: Amelia J. Betts. Kansas Ornithol. Soc. Bull. 36(2): 23–24.

Kelley, K., M. Boyd, R. Boyd, and C. Cink. 1981. Purple Finch returns – winter 1980 – 1981 – Baldwin City, Kansas. Inland Bird Banding 53: 14.

Kellogg, V. L. 1894. Notes on Kansas birds. Auk 11(3): 260.

Kennedy, E. D., and D. W. White. 1996. Interference competition from House Wrens as a factor in the decline of Bewick's Wrens. Conservation Biology 10(1): 281–284.

Kirn, A. J. 1916. Birds of Kansas farm-yard. The Oologist 33: 72 & 74.

Kirn, A. J. 1919. Second occurrence of the Painted Bunting at Solomon, Saline County, Kansas. Condor 21(6): 236.

Kreissler, T. 1999. In Memoriam: Theodore M. Sperry (1907–1995). Kansas Ornithol. Soc. Bull. 50(2): 21–22.

Kuehn, M. D. 2008. Remembering Marvin D. Schwilling (November 18, 1924–June 28, 2008). Kansas Ornithol. Soc. Bull. 59(3): 29–32.

Lane, H. H. 1947. A survey of fossils vertebrates of Kansas, Part IV, birds. Trans. Kansas Acad. Sci. 49(4): 390–400.

Langley, W. 2000. Changes in wintering crow populations in Kansas. Kansas Ornithol. Soc. Bull. 51(2): 21–22.

Lantz, D. E. 1896. An annotated list of birds found near Manhattan, Kansas. Trans. Kansas Acad. Sci. 14: 115–123.

Lantz, D. E. 1899. A Review of Kansas Ornithology. Part 1: The Bibliography of Kansas Birds. Trans. Kansas Acad. Sci. 16: 224–244.

Lantz, D. E. 1901. A list of birds seen in Dickinson County, Kansas, from August, 1898, to August, 1900. Trans. Kansas Acad. Sci. 17: 116–121.

LaShelle, D. L., and T. G. Shane. 2000. Christmas Bird Counts Completed in Kansas 1900–1948: The Early Audubon Society Years. The Horned Lark 27(4): 17–18

Leopold, A., T. M. Sperry, W. S. Feeney, and J. Catenhusen. 1943. Population turnover on a Wisconsin pheasant refuge. J. Wildl. Mgt. 7: 383–394.

Lewis, E., and E. Lewis. 1976. The breeding season in Mitchell County. Kansas Ornithol. Soc. Newsletter. 3(6): 1–3.

Ligon, J. S. 1961. New Mexico birds and where to find them. Univ. of New Mexico Press, Albuquerque. 360 pp.

Linsdale, J. 1927. Notes on Summer birds of southwestern Kansas. Auk 44: 47–58.

Linsdale, J. M. 1928. Some environmental relations of the birds of the Missouri River region. Wilson Bull. 40(3): 157–177.

Linsdale, J., and E. R. Hall. 1927. Notes on the birds of Douglas County, Kansas. Wilson Bull. 39: 91–105.

Long, W. S. 1935. Observations on the November birds of western Kansas. Univ. Kansas Sci. Bull. 22(12): 225–248.

Long, W. S. 1940. Check-list of Kansas birds. Trans. Kansas Acad. Sci. 43: 433–456.

Lungstrom, L. G. 1946. Comparative microscopic study of the proventriculus and duodenum of the Mourning Dove, Red-headed Woodpecker and meadowlark. M.S. Thesis, Kansas St. College, Manhattan. 42 pp.

Maccarone, A. D., J. N. Brzorad, and H. M. Stone. 2008. Characteristics and energetics of Great Egret and Snowy Egret foraging flights. Waterbirds 31(4): 541–549.

Martinez, E. F. 1979. Shorebird Banding at the Cheyenne Bottoms Waterfowl Management Area. Wader Study Group Bulletin No. 25: 40–41.

Mayr, E. 1975. Epilogue: Materials for a History of American Ornithology. In E. Stresemann. Ornithology from Aristole to the Present, 365–396. Translated by Hans J. and Cathleen Epstein. Edited by G. William Cottrell. Harvard University Press, Cambridge, Massachusetts.

Mead, J. R. 1899. Were quails native to Kansas? Trans. Kansas Acad. Sci. 16: 277–278.

Mead, J. R. 1986. Hunting and Trading on the Great Plains: 1859–1875. Univ. Oklahoma Press, Norman. 276 pp.

Mengel, R. M. 1965. The birds of Kentucky. Ornithol. Monogr. No. 3. AOU. 581 pp.

Mengel, R. M. 1970. The North American central plains as an isolating agent in bird speciation. In Pleistocene and recent environments of the central Great Plains, Department of Geology, University of Kansas Special Publication 3, 279–340. Univ. Press of Kansas, Lawrence.

Menke, H. W. 1894. List of birds of Finney County, Kansas. Kansas Univ. Quart. 3(2): 129–135.

Miller, R. F., and I. L. Boyd. 1947. Migration records of birds in East-central Kansas. Trans. Kansas Acad. Sci. 50(1): 62–71.

Mosby, L. D., and W. M. Lynn. 1956. Water birds resident in Kansas in summer, 1955. Trans. Kansas Acad. Sci. 59(4): 455–458.

Neudorf, D. L. H., R. A. Bodily, and T. G. Shane. (March 30, 2006). Lark Bunting (*Calamospiza melanocorys*): A technical conservation assessment. USDA Forest Service, Rocky Mountain Region. Online: http://www.fs.fed.us/r2/projects/scp/assessments/larkbunting.pdf

Nininger, H. H. 1927. A field guide to the birds of central Kansas. Democrat-Opinion Print, McPherson. 36 pp.

Nininger, H. H. 1928. The Bullock Oriole in Kansas. Trans. Kansas Acad. Sci. 31: 99. 36 pp.

Nonhof, A. G. 1980. A nesting study of the Pine Siskin (*Spinus pinus*) at Hays, Kansas. M. S. thesis, Fort Hays State University, Hays, Kansas. 28 pp. Online: http://contentcat.fhsu.edu/cdm/singleitem/collection/thesis/id/1868/rec/4

Nonhof, A. G. 1984. Note on movements of Kansas Pine Siskins. Kansas Ornithol. Soc. Bull. 35(2): 24.

Oehser, P. H. 1980. In Memoriam: Alexander Wetmore. Auk 97: 608–615.

Parmelee, D. F. 1980. Bird Island in the Antarctic Waters. University of Minnesota Press, Minneapolis, 140 pp.

Parmelee, D. F. 1992. Antarctic Birds: An Ecological and Behavioral Approach (Exploration of Palmer Archipelago by an Artist-Ornithologist). University of Minnesota Press, 203 pp.

Parmelee, D. F., M. D. Schwilling, and H. A. Stephens. 1969a. Charadriiform birds of Cheyenne Bottoms, Part I. Kansas Ornithol. Soc. Bull. 20(2): 9–13.

Parmelee, D. F., M. D. Schwilling, and H. A. Stephens. 1969b. Charadriiform birds of Cheyenne Bottoms, Part II. Kansas Ornithol. Soc. Bull. 20(3): 17–24.

Parmelee, D. F., H. A. Stephens, and R. H. Schmidt. 1967. The Birds of Southeastern Victoria Island and Adjacent Small Islands. National Museums of Canada, Ottawa 229 pp.

Patterson, J. 2008. An analysis of spring bird migration phenology in Kansas. M. A. Thesis, Kansas St. Univ., Manhattan, 90 pp. Online: http://krex.kstate.edu/dspace/bitstream/2097/646/3/JuddPatterson2008.pdf

Penner, R. L., II. 2009. The birds of Cheyenne Bottoms. Kansas Wildlife and Parks and The Nature Conservancy. 156 pp.

Peck, R. M. 1991. Robert M. Mengel (1921–1990): The blending of science and art. Wilson Bull. 103(3): 339–356.

Pike, Z. M. 1810. An account of expeditions to the sources of the Mississippi, and through the western parts of Louisiana to the sources of the Arkansaw, Kansas, La Platte and Pierre Juan Rivers, performed by the order of the government of the United States during the years 1805, 1806, and 1807. Philadelphia.

Pitelka, F. A. 1993. Academic tree for Loye and Alden Miller. Condor 95: 1065–1067.

Pittman, G. L. 1991. My 1990 birding Big Year in Kansas. The Horned Lark 18(2); 2–4.

Pittman, G. L., and E. A. Young. 2010. Henry S. Fitch. (1909–2009). Kansas Ornithol. Soc. Bull. 61(3): 25–27.

Platt, D. R. 1975. Breeding birds of Sand Prairie Natural History Reservation, Harvey County, Kansas. American Birds 29(6): 1146–1151.

Platt, D. R. 2002. Fifty years of early winter bird counts in Harvey County, Kansas. Kansas Ornithol. Soc. Bull. 54(2): 21–36.

Platt, D. R. 2007. The Ruths from Halstead: Early KOS members dedicated birders and record keepers. In C. K. Miller, Fall KOS meeting paper abstracts. The Horned Lark (KOSN) 34(4): 4–10.

Porter, J. M. 1951. Sight records of bird migration in north-central Kansas. Kansas Ornithol. Soc. Bull. 2(3): 21–26.

Prum, R. O. 2002. Why ornithologists should care about the Theropod origin of birds. Auk 119(1): 1–17.

Rader, M. 1999. Mike's Musings: Backing into a Big Year. The Horned Lark 26(1): 5–6.

Rader, M. 2002. Birding Kansas nets 225 species: Setting new state record, in one extraordinary day. Prairie Wings, Audubon of Kansas Newsletter, Fall 2002, pp. 1 & 21–23. Online: http://www.audubon-ofkansas.org/prairiewings/prairiewingsf02.pdf

Reed, B. P. 1922. Bird Catastrophe at Gordon, Nebraska. Wilson Bull. 39(3): 428.

Reed, B. P. 1927. Some observations in a Green Heron colony (*Butorides virescens*). Wilson Bull. 39(2): 81–85.

Rhodes, H. L. 1932. Bird Notes. Charles Hillebrandt, publisher, Wellington, Kansas. 223 pp.

Rice, O. 1968. In Memoriam: Lenwood B. Carson. Kansas Ornithol. Soc. Bull. 19(4): 21.

Rising, J. D. 1965. Summer birds from Cherokee County, Kansas. Kansas Ornithol. Soc. Bull. 16(2): 9–14.

Rising, J. D. 1974. The status and faunal affinities of the summer birds of western Kansas. Univ. Kansas Sci. Bull. 50(8): 347–388.

Robins, J. D., and G. L. Worthen. 1973. The Christmas Bird Counts in Kansas. Kansas Ornithol. Soc. Bull. 24(3): 17–30.

Robl, F. W. 1928. Duck Banding near the Cheyenne Bottoms, Kansas. Wilson Bull. 40(1): 58–59.

Roth, S. D., Jr., and J. M. Marzluff. 1989. Nest placement and productivity of Ferruginous Hawks in western Kansas. Trans. Kansas Acad. Sci. 92: 132–148.

Rowe, J. C. 1959. The ecology of the Ring-necked Pheasant (*Phasianus colchicus*, Linnaeus) in northwestern Kansas. M.S. Thesis. Kansas St. Univ., Manhattan. 64 pp.

Schulenberg, J. H., G. L. Horak, M. D. Schwilling, and E. J. Finck. 1994. Nesting of Henslow's Sparrow in Osage County, Kansas. Kansas Ornithol. Soc. Bull. 44 [sic], 45(3): 25–28.

Schulenberg, J. H., and M. B. Ptacek. 1984. Status of the Interior Least Tern in Kansas. American Birds 38(6): 975–981.

Schukman, J. M. 1993. Breeding ecology and distribution limits of phoebes in western Kansas. Kansas Ornithol. Soc. Bull. 44(3): 25–29.

Schukman, J. M. 1996. Temporal and spatial relationships of three canopy-dwelling warblers in a Missouri River bottomland. Kansas Ornithol. Soc. Bull. 47(4): 37–40.

Schwilling, M. D. 1955. A study of the Lesser Prairie Chicken in Kansas. A report to the Forestry Fish and Game Commission. 100 pp.

Schwilling, M. D. 1976. In Memoriam: Frank Robl. Inland Bird Banding News. 48(6): 203–204.

Schwilling, M. D. 1996. Backyard Birds. The Kansas School Naturalist 42(2); 16 pp.

Seibel, D. E. 1978. A Directory to the Birds of Cowley and Sumner Counties, Kansas, and the Chaplin Nature Center. Wichita, KS: Wichita Audubon Soc. Miscellaneous Publication No. 1. 74 pp.

Shane, T. G. 1972. The nest site selection behavior of the Lark Bunting, *Calamospiza melanocorys*. M.S. thesis, Kansas State University, Manhattan. Online: http://krex.k-state.edu/dspace/handle/2097/10615

Shane, T. G. 1998. A brief early history of the Manhattan, Kansas midwinter bird count. The Prairie Falcon 26(6): 3–4.

Shane, T. G., and E. M. Lewis. 1998. Arthur L. Goodrich: A Kansas Ornithological Society Founder. Kansas Ornithol. Soc. Bull. 49(4): 41–43.

Sharp, W., and P. Sullivan. 1990. The Dashing Kansan: Lewis Lindsay Dyche. Harrow Books, Kansas City, Missouri. 223 pp.

Sibley, C. G. 1955. Ornithology. 629–659. In A Century of Progress in the Natural Sciences 1853–1953. California Academy of Sciences, San Francisco.

Smith, R. C. 1931. F. F. Crevecoeur – A versatile naturalist 1862–1931. Trans. Kansas Acad. Sci. 34: 138–144.

Snow, F. H. 1871. The higher education of woman. The Kansas Educational Journal. 7(April): 307–321.

Snow, F. H. 1872. A catalogue of the birds of Kansas. Trans. Kansas Acad. Sci. 1: 21–29.

Snow, F. H. 1903. A catalogue of the birds of Kansas. Trans. Kansas Acad. Sci. 18: 154–176.

Stapanian, M. A., C. C. Smith, and E. J. Finck. 1999. The response of a Kansas winter bird community to weather, photoperiod, and year. Wilson Bull. 111(4): 550–557.

Stephens, H. A. 1980. The Great Blue Heron in Kansas. Trans. Kansas Acad. Sci. 83(4): 161–186.

Stevenson, M. 1969. Agonistic behavior in the cowbird *Molothrus ater*. PhD Dissertation, Kansas St. Univ., Manhattan. 46 pp.

Taylor, H. J., Mrs. 1932. Snow and Goss, The pioneers in Kansas Ornithology. Wilson Bull. 44(3): 158–169.

Tekiela, S. 2001. Birds of Kansas: Field Guide. Adventure Publications, Cambridge, Minnesota. 296 pp.

Terman, M. R. 1996. Messages from an Owl. Princeton University Press. 233 pp.

The Birds of North America. 2002. The Birds of North America: Cumulative Index Nos. 1–716. Philadelphia, PA.

Thompson, M. C. 1998. In Memoriam: E. Maurice Nuss. Kansas Ornithol. Soc. Bull. 49: 38–39.

Thompson, M. C., and C. Ely. 1989. Birds in Kansas. Vol. I. Univ. Kansas Mus. Nat. Hist. Publ. Ed. Ser. No. 11, xv + 404 pp.

Thompson, M. C., and C. Ely. 1992. Birds in Kansas. Vol. 2. Univ. Kansas Mus. Nat. Hist. Publ. Ed. Ser. No. 12. 422 pp.

Tiemeier, O. W. 1938. Summer birds of Rawlins County, Kansas. Trans. Kansas Acad. Sci. 40: 397–399.

Tiemeier, O. W. 1941. Repaired bone injuries in birds. Auk 58: 350–359.

Timson, J. E., and G. H. Farley. 2003. Intraspecific helping behavior exhibited by hatch-year house wren. Southwestern Nat. 48(2): 300–301.

Tordoff, H. B. 1956. Check-list of the birds of Kansas. Univ. Kansas Publ. Mus. Nat. Hist. 8: 307–359.

Tordoff, H. B. 1991. In Memoriam: Robert M. Mengel. Auk 108: 161–165.

Trigg, I. H. 1951. Some observations of the ecology of the Ring-necked Pheasant in Hamilton County, Kansas. M.S. Thesis Kansas St. College, Manhattan. 33 pp.

Watkins, M. A., and D. W. Mulhern. 1999. Ten years of successful Bald Eagle nesting in Kansas. Kansas Ornithol. Soc. Bull. 50(3): 29–33.

Wells, W. 1940. Birds breeding in Anderson County, Kansas. The Oologist 57: 50–53.

Wetmore, A. 1909. Fall notes from eastern Kansas. Condor 11: 154–164.

Williams, J. G. 1933. A survey and census of the birds of Crawford County Kansas. M. S. thesis, Kansas State Teachers College, Pittsburg, Kansas, 158 pp.

Wilson, E. O. 1975. Sociobiology. Belknap Press, Cambridge, Massachusetts. 697 pp.

Wilson, F. E., and B. D. Reinert. 2000. Thyroid hormone acts centrally to programme photostimulated male American tree sparrows (*Spizella arborea*) for vernal and autumnal components of seasonality. Journal of Neuroendocrinology 12: 87–95.

Winker, K. 1999. In Memoriam: David F. Parmelee, 1924–1998. Auk 116(3): 816–817.

Wolfe, L. R. 1961. The breeding birds of Decatur County, Kansas: 1908–1915. Kansas Ornithol. Soc. Bull. 12(4): 27–30.

Wooster, L. D. 1925. Nature Studies (Animals). Kansas St. Teachers College of Hays Bulletin. 15(4): 1–75.

Young, E. A. 1993. A survey of the vertebrates of Slate Creek Salt Marsh, Sumner County, Kansas with an emphasis on water birds. M.S. Thesis, Fort Hays State University, Hays, Kansas. 187 pp. Online: http://cdm15732.contentdm.oclc.org/utils/getfile/collection/thesis/id/2970/filename/2971.pdf

Young, J. R., C. E. Braun, S. J. Oyler-McCance, J. W. Hupp, and T. W. Quinn. 2000. A new species of sage-grouse (Phasianidae: *Centrocerus*) from southwestern Colorado. Wilson Bull. 112(4): 445–453.

Zimmerman, J. L. 1978. Ten year summary of the Kansas Breeding Bird Survey: An overview. Kansas Ornithol. Soc. Bull. 29(4): 26–31.

Zimmerman, J. L. 1990. Cheyenne Bottoms: Wetland in Jeopardy. University Press of Kansas, Lawrence. 197 pp.

Zimmerman, J. L. 1993. The Birds of Konza: The Avian Ecology of the Tallgrass Prairie. Univ. Press of Kansas, Kansas. 186 pp.

Zimmerman, J. L. 1998. Migration of Birds, 3rd ed. U.S. Fish and Wildlife Service. Circular 16. 113 pp.

Zimmerman, J. L., and S. Patti. 1988. A Guide to Bird Finding in Kansas and Western Missouri. University Press of Kansas, Lawrence. 244 pp.

Zuvanich, J. R., and M. G. McHenry. 1964. Comparison of water birds observed in Kansas in 1955 and 1963. Trans. Kansas Acad. Sci. 67(1):169–183.

About the Author

From the age of 5 ½ when he identified his first bird, a male Rose-breasted Grosbeak, in a Seneca, Kansas alley during the summer of 1951, Tom Shane has always been a student of Great Plains birds. He attended Kansas State University where he received a Bachelor's and a Master's degree in Environmental Biology. He worked in the recycling and remanufacturing fields as a manufacturer's agent for 25 years. He is a past president of the Kansas Ornithological Society, and the author of the Lark Bunting profile for The Birds of North America sponsored by Cornell, AOU and The Academy of Natural Sciences. He is a member of the Kansas, Oklahoma and Texas ornithological societies, plus the Nebraska Ornithologists' Union and is a member of all six national ornithological organizations. After retiring he has been tutoring at the Garden City Community College library, and working for a NIH program with minority students on bird research. He and his wife Sara, also an avid bird watcher, reside in Garden City, Kansas.